W9-CLR-654

pybnf
523.1 WOOD

Wood, Matthew Brenden, author
The universe
33410017115330          05-04-2021

DISCARD
PORTER COUNTY
LIBRARY SYSTEM

# THE

**THE BIG BANG, BLACK HOLES, AND BLUE WHALES**

# UNIVERSE

**MATTHEW BRENDEN WOOD**
Illustrated by Alexis Cornell

Nomad Press

A division of Nomad Communications

10 9 8 7 6 5 4 3 2 1

Copyright © 2021 by Nomad Press. All rights reserved.

No part of this book may be reproduced in any form without permission in writing from the publisher, except by a reviewer who may quote brief passages in a review or **for limited educational use**. The trademark "Nomad Press" and the Nomad Press logo are trademarks of Nomad Communications, Inc.

This book was manufactured by CGB Printers,
North Mankato, Minnesota, United States
April 2021, Job #1018038

ISBN Softcover: 978-1-61930-932-6
ISBN Hardcover: 978-1-61930-929-6

Educational Consultant, Marla Conn

Questions regarding the ordering of this book should be addressed to
Nomad Press
2456 Christian St., White River Junction, VT 05001
www.nomadpress.net

Printed in the United States.

More space science titles from the Inquire & Investigate series.

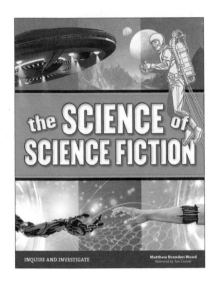

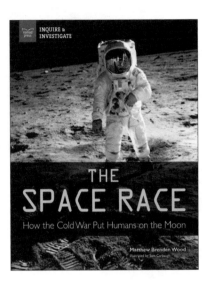

Check out more titles at www.nomadpress.net

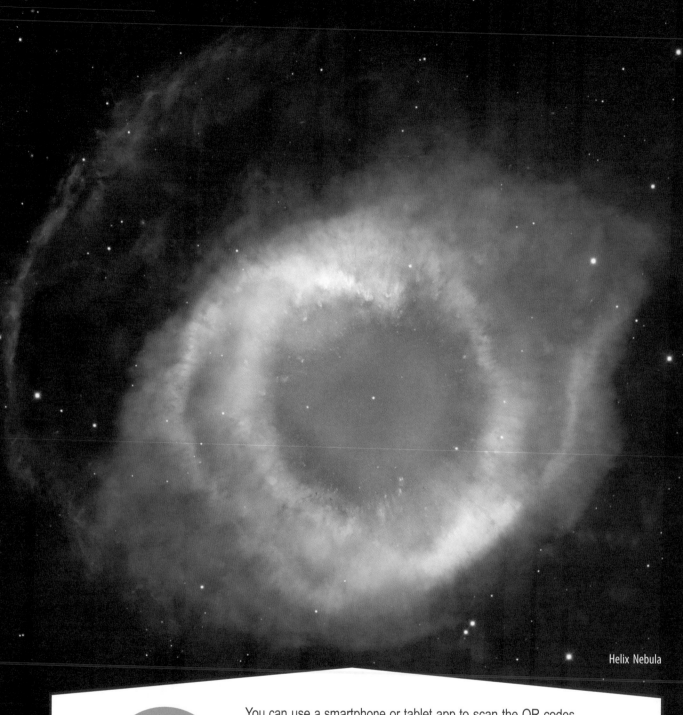

Helix Nebula

Interested in primary sources?

**PS**

**Look for this icon.**

You can use a smartphone or tablet app to scan the QR codes and explore more! Cover up neighboring QR codes to make sure you're scanning the right one. You can find a list of URLs on the Resources page.

If the QR code doesn't work, try searching the internet with the Keyword Prompts to find other helpful sources.

🔍 universe origins

# Contents

Glossary ▼ Resources
Selected Bibliography ▼ Index

# TIMELINE

| YEARS AGO | EVENT (age of the universe) | universe | earth | life |
|---|---|---|---|---|
| 13.8 billion years | (0) THE BIG BANG, when space begins to stretch and expand all at once in every direction | | | |
| 13.8 billion years | ($10^{-43}$ seconds) The universe is almost infinitely hot and dense, but is already expanding and cooling | | | |
| 13.8 billion years | ($10^{-36}$ seconds) The fundamental forces of nature begin to separate from each other | | | |
| 13.8 billion years | ($10^{-32}$ seconds) Cosmic inflation causes space to expand faster than light | | | |
| 13.8 billion years | ($10^{-6}$ seconds) The first elementary particles appear in the universe, including quarks and gluons | | | |
| 13.8 billion years | (1 second) Quarks come together to form protons and neutrons | | | |
| 13.8 billion years | (10 seconds) Most particles and antiparticles annihilate each other, leaving only particles | | | |
| 13.8 billion years | (20 minutes) The first atomic nuclei of hydrogen, helium, and lithium form | | | |
| 13 billion years | (380,000 years) The first light appears in the universe, visible today as cosmic microwave background radiation | | | |
| 12.6 billion years | (100–400 million years) The first stars and galaxies form, including the Milky Way | | | |
| 4.57 billion years | (9.2 billion years) The sun and solar system form | | | |
| 4.53 billion years | The moon forms when a Mars-sized object collides with Earth | | | |
| 4.4 billion years | Oceans form on Earth | | | |
| 4.2 billion years | The earliest life could have formed on Earth | | | |
| 4.1 billion years | Late Heavy Bombardment begins, when the inner planets are pummeled by debris leftover from the formation of the solar system | | | |
| 3.9 billion years | Oldest fossil evidence of life | | | |
| 3.8 billion years | Late Heavy Bombardment ends, oceans form | | | |
| 3.5 billion years | The last ancestor of all living things splits into bacteria and archaea | | | |
| 2.7 billion years | The first eukaryotes appear | | | |
| 2.5 billion years | Cyanobacteria first perform photosynthesis, releasing oxygen into the atmosphere | | | |
| 2.1 billion years | The first multicellular life forms | | | |
| 1.9 billion years | Oxygen makes up 15 percent of the atmosphere | | | |
| 1.8 billion years | Supercontinent Columbia forms | | | |
| 1.5 billion years | Supercontinent Columbia breaks up | | | |
| 1.2 billion years | Supercontinent Rhodinia forms | | | |
| 750 million years | Supercontinent Rhodinia breaks up | | | |
| 540 million years | The Cambrian Explosion begins, when life becomes incredibly diverse | | | |
| 440 million years | The first plants and animals arrive on land | | | |
| 445 million years | 70 percent of all species go extinct in the Late Devonian Extinction | | | |
| 310 million years | The first reptiles appear | | | |
| 300 million years | Supercontinent Pangaea forms | | | |
| 251 million years | The Permian extinction occurs, when more than 90 percent of all species go extinct | | | |
| 230 million years | The first dinosaurs appear | | | |
| 200 million years | The first mammals appear | | | |
| 201 million years | The Triassic extinction occurs, when more than 75 percent of all species go extinct | | | |
| 180 million years | Supercontinent Pangaea splits into Laurasia and Gondwana | | | |
| 155 million years | The first birds appear | | | |

| YEARS AGO | EVENT (age of the universe) | universe | earth | life |
|---|---|---|---|---|
| 90 million years | India splits from Gondwana | | | |
| 80 million years | Australia splits from Antarctica | | | |
| 68 million years | The Tyrannosaurus Rex appears | | | |
| 66 million years | The Chicxulub asteroid impact kills 75 percent of all species on Earth, including the dinosaurs, but mammals survive | | | |
| 55 million | The first primates appear | | | |
| 6 million years | Last common ancestor of chimpanzees and humans | | | |
| 4 million years | Australopithecus, ancient ancestor of humans, appears | | | |
| 1.5 million years | The first evidence of fire used by Homo erectus, an ancestor of modern humans | | | |
| 250,000 years | Denisovans and Neanderthals appear | | | |
| 195,000 years | The first modern humans appear | | | |
| 40,000 years | Denisovans and Neanderthals go extinct | | | |
| 50 years | The first humans walk on the moon | | | |
| Present | This book is published. | | | |
| in 100,000 years | Constellations in the sky will be unrecognizable | | | |
| 300,000 years | The carbon dioxide in the atmosphere returns to pre-industrial levels | | | |
| 300,000 years | *Voyager 2*, the furthest spacecraft from Earth, passes within 4.3 light years of the star Sirius | | | |
| 15 million years | East Africa splits from Africa | | | |
| 50 million years | Africa collides with Eurasia | | | |
| 100 million years | Saturn's rings are gone | | | |
| 240 million years | The solar system will have completed one orbit around the Milky Way | | | |
| 1.1 billion years | The sun's increased energy output makes Earth too hot to support life | | | |
| 2 billion years | Earth's oceans evaporate | | | |
| 4.5 billion years | Andromeda and the Milky Way collide, merging to form a giant elliptical galaxy called Milkdromeda | | | |
| 5 billion years | The sun runs out of hydrogen in its core and becomes a red giant star, eventually swallowing Mercury, Venus, and maybe Earth | | | |
| 8 billion years | The sun throws off its outer layers and becomes a white dwarf star | | | |
| 50 billion years | Earth becomes tidally locked with the moon, and a day on Earth will last 47 days | | | |
| 100 billion years | The universe expands so much that all but the nearest galaxies have disappeared from view | | | |
| 450 billion years | All nearby galaxies will have merged with Milkdromeda into a giant supergalaxy | | | |
| 1 trillion years | The sun becomes a black dwarf, and only red dwarf stars are still shining | | | |
| 3 trillion years | All distant galaxies will have disappeared from view, and the cosmic background radiation—the echo of the Big Bang—will have faded away | | | |
| 100 trillion years | The last stars in the universe become black dwarfs, leaving the universe cold and dark | | | |
| 10^21 years | The black dwarf remnant of the sun will have collided with another black dwarf, destroying the solar system or ejecting out of the galaxy | | | |
| 10^30 years | Protons stars to decay, breaking apart | | | |
| 10^100 years | Black holes evaporate | | | |
| Beyond | The temperature of the universe cools to nearly absolute zero | | | |

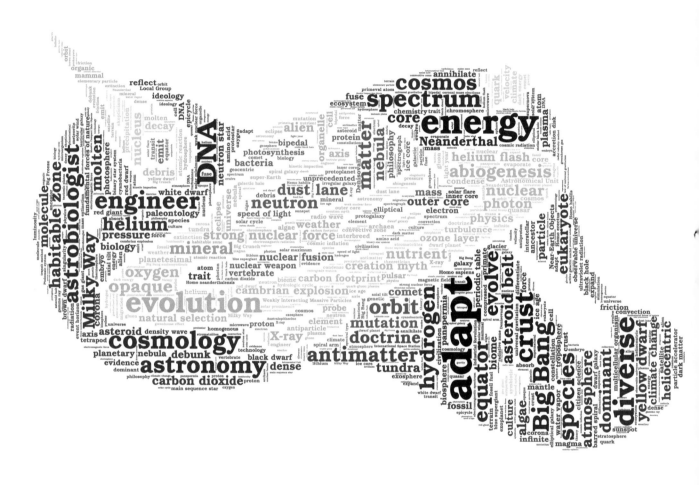

# Introduction ▶
# Welcome to the Universe

How did the
universe begin?

Since humans first evolved, people have wondered how the universe began. As science and technology became more precise, scientists and other thinkers have been able to put forth logical theories with supporting evidence—but there is still plenty we don't know!

● ● ● ● ● ● ● ●

**Have you ever wondered where the universe came from? Did it have a beginning? Will it have an end? Where did all the stuff—the stars, galaxies, planets, people, and everything else—come from? These are the kinds of questions that cosmologists work to answer.**

Cosmology is the study of the evolution of the universe—how it got its start, what it's like today, and what it will be like in the future. That's a pretty enormous topic!

Cosmologists use many different tools and branches of science to help them answer these big questions. Like astronomers, cosmologists use telescopes to view the most ancient and distant objects in the universe. Like physicists, they work with machines such as particle accelerators to unlock the secrets of the tiniest bits of matter and energy around us. And like theoreticians, they use mathematics to explore the parts of the universe that can't be observed or measured directly.

Despite modern tools, cosmology isn't a new science. In fact, as with astronomy, it's one of the oldest sciences in the world. For thousands of years, people have looked at the world around them and tried to explain what they saw. Most ancient cultures told creation myths—stories and legends to explain how and why the universe came to be. Many featured incredible tales of gods and goddesses who created the cosmos and everything in it.

> Lots of these stories had the earth and people at the center of everything. But, as our understanding of math and science changed, so did our views of the universe.

Today, we know the universe is mind-bogglingly huge. The earth, our sun, and even our galaxy exist in just a tiny and unremarkable part of a cosmos filled with more galaxies than we can count. But humans haven't always accepted this as truth. For thousands of years, people thought the universe was much smaller and that the earth had a much more important position than we believe it does today.

## THE GEOCENTRIC UNIVERSE

Do you know someone who thinks the whole universe revolves around them? It might seem a little selfish to us, but to the ancient Greeks, it made perfect sense to put themselves and the earth at the center of the universe. After all, they had no telescopes to examine the planets up close and no satellites with which to gaze at the earth from a distance. As far as they could tell, the earth under their feet was motionless while the rest of the cosmos circled overhead.

What is the universe? The universe is everything around us. It's everything we can sense, measure, or detect. That includes planets, stars, galaxies, matter and energy, time and space—even you!

● ● ● ● ● ● ● ● ●

## COSMIC CONCEPT

Sir Isaac Newton (1642–1727) was an English physicist and mathematician and one of the most important scientists in history. His three laws of motion led to his discovery of the law of universal gravitation, which explained that the force that causes things to fall on Earth is the same force that keeps planets in their orbits around the sun.

The Ptolemaic geocentric model of the universe, drawn by Portuguese cosmographer and cartographer Bartolomeu Velho, 1568

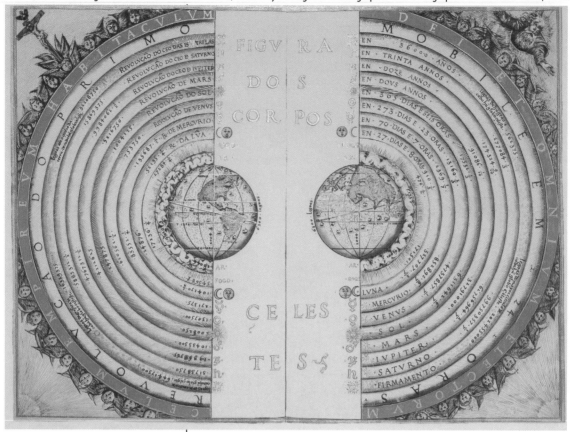

## COSMIC CONCEPT

One of the first people to make the geocentric model of the universe popular was Aristotle (384–322 BCE). Aristotle was a Greek mathematician and philosopher whose writings have influenced science, philosophy, and religion for more than 2,000 years.

From these observations they created a geocentric model of the universe in which the sun, moon, planets, and stars all circled the earth on perfect and invisible cosmic spheres.

While this model was hugely popular, it had a few big problems. For one, people watching the skies noticed that the planets seemed to change in brightness over time, which didn't make sense if they always circled Earth at the same distance. Plus, the planets occasionally appeared to slow down and move backward in the sky before turning around.

This retrograde motion baffled astronomers for centuries.

An Egyptian astronomer named Claudius Ptolemy (85–165 CE) came along and offered a fix. After carefully observing and recording the motion of the planets, Ptolemy came up with a solution that neatly explained the strange motions.

In Ptolemy's system, as each planet circled the earth it also moved in a smaller circle called an epicycle.

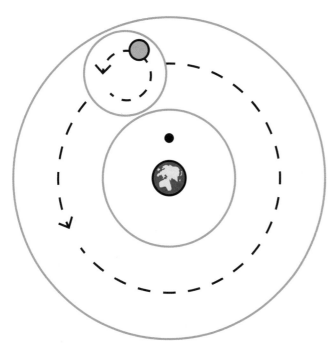

By adding these epicycles, Ptolemy was able to predict planetary motions with an accuracy that nobody could beat. With this fix, the Ptolemaic model kept the universe centered on the earth for more than a thousand years. It became so popular that powerful religious authorities such as the Catholic Church adopted it and used it in their teachings. However, just because it worked didn't mean it was right.

## SCIENTIFIC METHOD

The scientific method is the process scientists use to ask questions and find answers. Keep a science journal to record your methods and observations during all the activities in this book. You can use a scientific method worksheet to keep your ideas and observations organized.

**Question:** What are we trying to find out? What problem are we trying to solve?

**Research:** What is already known about this topic?

**Hypothesis:** What do we think the answer will be?

**Equipment:** What supplies are we using?

**Method:** What procedure are we following?

**Results:** What happened and why?

# HERE COMES THE SUN: THE HELIOCENTRIC UNIVERSE

As the centuries went on and measurements became more precise, the Ptolemaic system started to show its age. By the sixteenth century, planets were in the wrong place, eclipses were off, and astronomers were getting frustrated.

In 1504, a Polish astronomer named Nicolaus Copernicus (1473–1543) thought he could do better. Feeling Ptolemy's system of epicycles was too complicated, Copernicus looked for a simpler solution to explain the backward motion of the planets.

His idea was to place the sun at the center, with the earth in motion around it as if it were just another planet. Copernicus's heliocentric system neatly explained the backward motion of planets as the effect of Earth passing another planet as both moved around the sun—not epicycles.

## PRIMARY SOURCES

PS

Primary sources come from people who were eyewitnesses to events. They might write about the event, take pictures, post short messages to social media or blogs, or record the event for radio or video. The photographs in this book are primary sources, taken at the time of the event. Paintings of events are usually not primary sources, since they were often painted long after the event took place.

What other primary sources can you find? Why are primary sources important? Do you learn differently from primary sources than from secondary sources, which come from people who did not directly experience the event?

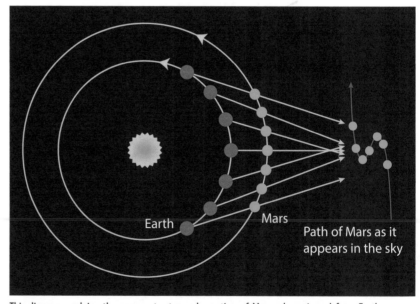

This diagram explains the apparent retrograde motion of Mars when viewed from Earth.

Credit: Wellcome Images, a website operated by Wellcome Trust (CC BY 4.0)

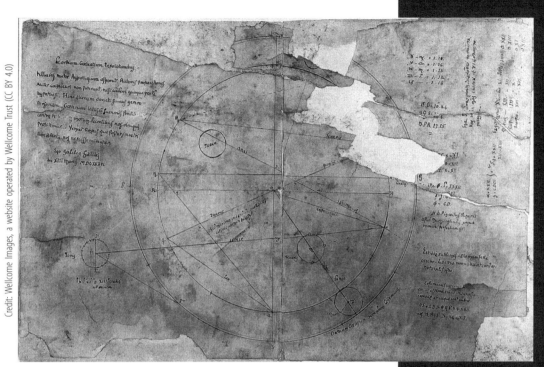

An astronomical drawing by Galileo, 1636

Once published, Copernicus's model didn't catch on right away.

There was a lot of resistance from the Catholic Church, which had a great influence on Western society at the time. But evidence that Copernicus was on to something began to pile up.

In 1610, the famous Italian astronomer Galileo Galilee (1564–1642) found the first direct proof that the earth was not the center of the universe. By pointing the newly invented telescope to the sky, he watched as Venus went through phases in the same way as the moon—something that could only happen if Venus circled the sun. He was also the first person to see the moons of Jupiter, proving that not everything in the cosmos circled the earth.

Copernicus, afraid of ridicule by his peers, waited until the end of his life to publish his heliocentric model in *De revolutionibus orbium coelestium* (*On the Revolutions of the Heavenly Spheres*). He didn't live to see how his ideas changed the world. Learn more about Copernicus and his life here.

**PS**

Biography
Copernicus video

## SORRY!

While Galileo and many other astronomers were convinced of a heliocentric universe, the powerful Catholic Church was not. The church had taught that the earth was the center of the universe for centuries, and felt that a sun-centered universe challenged its power. Galileo was punished and forced to stay in his home under house arrest until he died in 1642. It took until 1822 for the church to officially accept heliocentrism, and it wasn't until 1992 that Galileo was officially forgiven! You can read a news article about it here. Why do you think it took so long for the church to admit Galileo was right?

 NYT Vatican Galileo

Around the same time Galileo was looking through his telescope, Johannes Kepler (1571–1630) discovered the laws of planetary motion, which described how the planets move in their orbits around the sun. This work let astronomers understand and predict the motions of the planets with more accuracy than ever before.

Among these astronomers was Isaac Newton, one of the greatest scientists of all time. He managed to unlock the laws of motion and gravity to show that the same forces keeping things on Earth also kept planets moving in their orbits around the sun.

In the face of all this evidence, most scholars agreed the sun had to be the center of the universe. It turned out, they were only half right.

## A COSMIC SHIFT

By the end of the nineteenth century, the view of the universe had changed again. The sun was no longer the center of the cosmos but just one star in a sea of billions that make up the Milky Way. A great debate was raging about strange objects called spiral nebulae. Some astronomers believed they were "island universes," similar to our galaxy, while others argued they could exist outside our home galaxy.

In 1925, astronomer Edwin Hubble (1889–1953) solved the debate. He'd measured the distance to the Andromeda Nebula and found it to be more than 2.5 billion light years away—a distance that proved it was an island universe of its own: the Andromeda Galaxy. Suddenly, the Milky Way was just one galaxy out of many and the universe had grown tremendously in size.

The Andromeda Galaxy

Hubble's most important discovery came a few years later, when he realized that, not only were almost all these galaxies moving away from us at a great speed, but also the greater their distance, the faster their speed. Astronomers around the world struggled to understand what this meant.

Until Hubble's discovery, the universe was considered a static, unchanging place. But now it was obvious that galaxies everywhere were racing away from us in all directions. What did it mean?

It turned out that a previously unknown physicist and priest named Georges Lemaître (1894–1966) had already figured out the answer. Lemaître had studied Albert Einstein's (1879–1955) famous work on general relativity, which describes how space itself can be bent and stretched. Lemaître found that Einstein's ideas predicted a universe that was growing and stretching, carrying galaxies away from each other as space itself expanded in all directions.

## FUNDAMENTAL FORCES

The four fundamental forces of nature are like the universe's rulebook for matter and energy.

- Gravity is the familiar force that holds planets in their orbits and keeps us from flying off into space. Despite having a big influence on our lives, it's the weakest force.

- The electromagnetic force is related to electricity and magnetism. Without it, we wouldn't have electricity, refrigerator magnets or even light.

- The strong nuclear force holds together the particles that make up matter in the universe. Without the strong force, no atoms would exist, and without atoms, the universe would be a pretty boring place.

- The weak nuclear force helps break apart, or decay, particles, by emitting radiation. Without it, we wouldn't have nuclear fusion, the power source of stars.

Want to learn more about how these forces work? Check out this video.

 SciShow Fundamental Forces

> **Hubble discovered that, for galaxies, the greater the distance away they are, the greater their velocity away from us—and each other!**

• • • • • • •

**KEY QUESTIONS**

• Why are people sometimes resistant to new ideas?

• What are some other widely held theories that were debunked in your time? What was the process like?

• Is it important to know the origins of the universe?

It took other scientists years to accept Lemaître's idea, but in the end, they all agreed he was right. However, there was more to Lemaître's view of the universe. He also reasoned that if things in the universe were moving farther away from each other, they must have been closer together in the past. And if you kept moving back in time, then everything in the universe must have been mashed together in an unimaginably small and dense space from which the universe began in a burst of time and space. He called this hot and dense state the "primeval atom" and its sudden growth and expansion a "big noise."

> Like most things that change the world, Lemaître's vision of the universe was met with a lot of skepticism.

British astronomer Fred Hoyle (1915–2001), who didn't like the idea of a growing and changing universe, sarcastically called it the "Big Bang." And the name stuck.

The Big Bang didn't answer all the questions about the universe. In fact, it added new ones. How did the universe get started? How did stars, planets, and galaxies form? Where do we and our planet fit into everything? And if the universe had a beginning, will it have an end?

In *The Universe* you'll get to explore the latest scientific theories and discoveries concerning the universe, starting with the Big Bang. You'll learn about the life cycle of stars and the growth of galaxies, the formation of Earth and the rise of life. We'll even examine the possible fates of the solar system, our galaxy, and the universe itself.

The universe is a big place, so let's get started!

# INVESTIGATE A CREATION MYTH

Nearly all civilizations had their own creation myths. Sometimes, these creation myths were weirdly similar, even if the cultures had no known contact. Let's take a look at some and see if there is any truth in the stories.

- **Research a creation myth.** If you already know one or more, try to find one you're not familiar with! Head to the library or search online to find them.

- **Think about the following questions.**

  - How does the culture represent the universe? Do they use people, animals, or supernatural beings such as gods and goddesses?

  - According to the myth, how was the world or universe created?

  - Where did people come from?

  - How old is the earth?

  - How does the myth describe the way people and nature relate to each other?

To investigate more, compare two or more creation myths. What are the similarities and differences? Do they seem connected in some way? Create a representation of a creation myth using any materials you choose. It can be a web page, a diagram, or a model—whichever method you think will best represent the myth.

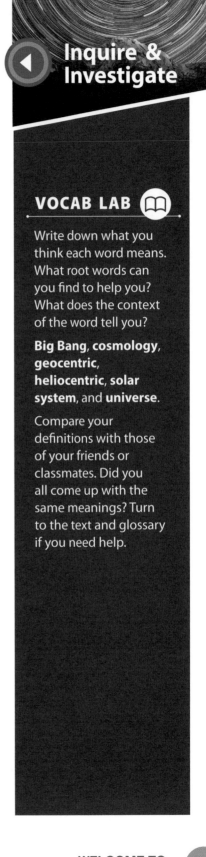

## VOCAB LAB

Write down what you think each word means. What root words can you find to help you? What does the context of the word tell you?

**Big Bang**, **cosmology**, **geocentric**, **heliocentric**, **solar system**, and **universe**.

Compare your definitions with those of your friends or classmates. Did you all come up with the same meanings? Turn to the text and glossary if you need help.

# Chapter 1 ▶
# It Begins With a Bang

IF THERE USED TO BE NOTHING, THEN WHERE DID EVERYTHING COME FROM?

Why is the Big Bang such a big deal?

At the beginning of the Big Bang, the entire universe was hotter and denser than even the biggest, hottest stars around today!

● ● ● ● ● ● ● ●

**Have you heard of the Big Bang? The Big Bang is the name of the scientific theory that best explains how the universe grew from an almost impossibly hot and dense state to the star-studded, galaxy-filled, and spied-upon-by-humans place it is today.**

Although it sounds like it was the greatest explosion of all time and space, the Big Bang wasn't a gigantic, thunderous fireball like you see in video games or movies. In fact, it wasn't an explosion at all. The Big Bang was a sudden expansion of space and time everywhere, all at once, in all directions. In other words, it was the beginning of the universe as we know it.

But stars and kitchen tables didn't pop into the universe fully assembled. The Big Bang set in motion a series of events that, during billions of years, led to the simplest, smallest atoms, the biggest spiral galaxies, and, on at least one planet, life. The Big Bang was a pretty big deal, and like many important things, it started out small.

# BLOWING UP: INFLATION

About 13.8 billion years ago, the universe was a very different place. Everything we see today, what astronomers call the observable universe, was crammed into an area billions of times smaller than any atom and trillions of times hotter than the hottest star.

There were no stars, galaxies, cats, or Wi-Fi back then. It was so hot and dense that even atoms, the building blocks of everything from bacteria to blue whales, didn't exist. Elementary particles, the tiniest bits of matter and energy in the universe, popped into and out of existence like bubbles in a pot of boiling water. Matter and energy were inseparable, a mixture of ultra-high-energy particles and radiation more intense than anything that has existed since.

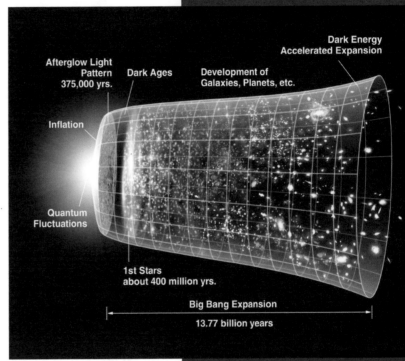

Even the fundamental forces of nature—gravity, the electromagnetic force, and both the strong and weak nuclear forces—were probably twisted together into a single super force. Thankfully for us, it didn't stay that way.

In the first tiny fraction of a second after the Big Bang, the four fundamental forces of nature began to separate. First came gravity, followed by the strong nuclear force, the electromagnetic force, and finally the weak nuclear force.

## BY THE NUMBERS

Scientists think that just seconds after the Big Bang, the earliest moment in time our understanding of physics allows us to calculate, the observable universe was just 10 billion trillion trillionths of an inch wide and about 100 million trillion trillion kelvin.

## REALLY HOT TEMPERATURES

When it comes to measuring really hot temperatures, astronomers use the kelvin temperature scale, named after its inventor, Lord Kelvin (1824–1907). For example, 0 kelvin is -459.67 degrees Fahrenheit—also known as absolute zero, the coldest possible temperature!

## THE QUIRKS OF QUARKS

There are six different types, or flavors, of quarks, and they come in pairs: up, down, top, bottom, strange, and charm. Up and down quarks come together to form protons and neutrons. The other flavors form rare and exotic particles. To learn more about quarks, check out this video.

🔍 Physics Girl quarks

These forces of nature determined how matter and energy should behave. Their arrival also triggered a sudden and tremendous growth spurt that cosmologists call cosmic inflation. In a very brief moment, space expanded faster than the speed of light, growing 100 trillion trillion times bigger, to about the size of a basketball, in 100 billion billionths of a second.

Just as quickly as it started, cosmic inflation ended, and the universe went back to expanding at a more leisurely pace. But that cosmic inflation dramatically cooled the universe. Just as cooling air causes water vapor to condense into raindrops and snowflakes, the first particles began to condense from the cooling sea of dense, ultra-hot energy.

## A STRANGE SOUP

Once temperatures in the early universe fell below 1 trillion kelvin (1.8 trillion degrees Fahrenheit), the first elementary particles appeared. Among the earliest to arrive were quarks and their sticky partners, gluons.

Quarks are a type of elementary particle and the smallest bits of matter in the universe. Today, they're joined together by gluons to make protons and neutrons, which form the nuclei of all atoms. But when they first appeared in the universe, it was too hot for gluons and quarks to make anything. Instead, the universe was filled with a weird, hot soup of quarks, gluons, and radiation—physicists call this a quark-gluon plasma.

A proton, formed by two up quarks and one down quark held together by gluons

A plasma is a state of matter that is a little like a gas, but is much too hot for particles to stick together and form anything bigger. When temperatures dropped to around 10 billion kelvin (18 billion degrees Fahrenheit), this strange quark soup became more like a stew. Just before the universe turned one second old, gluons started gluing quarks together to make the first protons and neutrons. But, before these heavier particles could come together to form atoms, they found themselves in an epic battle for their very existence—matter against antimatter!

## A COSMIC BATTLE ROYALE

When the first particles appeared in the universe, they weren't alone. Along with them came their evil twins, antiparticles. Antiparticles are just like regular particles but have an opposite electrical charge.

> For example, protons have a positive charge, while their antimatter twins, antiprotons, have a negative charge.

It might not seem like much, but this small difference can cause big problems. When a particle and its antiparticle meet, they annihilate each other with a spectacular burst of pure energy.

For several intense seconds, the battle between these rival particle gangs raged throughout the universe as pairs of particles and antiparticles annihilated each other almost as quickly as they formed. Had they been made in equal numbers, the battle would have ended only when every particle was annihilated, leaving the universe empty. Stars and galaxies would never have formed—and neither would you.

The periodic table arranges elements by the number of protons in their nuclei. Hydrogen, which has just one proton, is the simplest element and comes first. It's followed by helium, which has two protons, and then lithium, which has three, and so on. To learn more about the periodic table, check out this link.

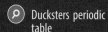 Ducksters periodic table

## WHAT'S THE MATTER WITH ANTIMATTER?

Have you heard of antimatter? Science fiction stories often use antimatter as fuel to power spaceships, but antimatter is not just science fiction. Antiprotons, antineutrons, and positrons (antielectrons) can come together to form antimatter atoms. If you had enough antimatter, you could even make antimatter stars or antimatter people! However, you wouldn't want to shake hands with your antimatter counterpart—that would be the end of both of you. Fortunately, antimatter is a little hard to find these days.

To learn more about antiparticles and antimatter, check out this video!

Seeker antimatter

For reasons scientists still don't understand, the number of particles in the early universe was slightly greater than the number of antiparticles. When the cosmic dust had settled, almost all the antiparticles were gone and only a tiny fraction of the regular particles remained. Those veteran particles, having survived a great cosmic battle, would eventually become all the matter in the universe we have today, including stars, planets, and even you. But it would be a while before that could happen.

## ATOMIC NUCLEI—DONE!

Just 10 seconds after the Big Bang, temperatures dropped below 1 billion kelvin (1.8 billion degrees Fahrenheit) and things began to come together. Protons and neutrons, slamming into each other with tremendous energy, began fusing in a process called Big Bang nucleosynthesis. The universe quickly began to fill with atomic nuclei, which form the center, or nucleus, of atoms.

The atomic nuclei of the element hydrogen, usually made from a single proton (and occasionally a proton and neutron together), made up about 75 percent of all the nuclei. Helium nuclei, usually two protons and two neutrons, made up about 25 percent, and lithium, which usually has three protons and three neutrons, made up less than 1 percent.

Only 20 minutes after the Big Bang, the ever-expanding and cooling universe had grown too cold for nucleosynthesis to continue, and the creation of atomic nuclei stopped. Heavier elements were nowhere to be found. In fact, all other elements on the periodic table, such as the oxygen we breathe and the iron in our blood, wouldn't be formed for hundreds of millions of years.

In less time than it takes to bake a frozen pizza, space went from a seething, hot realm to a universe filled with atomic nuclei in a sea of electrons and photons. But, it was still missing something—light.

# THE FLASH

Light is everywhere these days. The visible spectrum, the light that our eyes can detect, is just a tiny slice of the entire electromagnetic spectrum. The electromagnetic spectrum is the range of all the electromagnetic radiation, or light, in the universe. And from radio waves to gamma rays, light is the most powerful tool scientists have when studying the cosmos.

## COSMIC CONCEPT

The Big Bang theory can't tell us what the universe was like before the Big Bang or why it started expanding in the first place. That's because our current understanding of physics breaks down under the nearly infinite temperatures and pressures that must have been around when the Big Bang got going!

## ELECTROMAGNETIC SPECTRUM

| | | | | | | | |
|---|---|---|---|---|---|---|---|
| Sources | FM TV | Microwave Oven | TV Remote | Light Bulb | Sun | X-ray Machine | Radioactive Elements |
| | Radio | Microwaves | Infrared | Visible Light | Ultraviolet | X-rays | Gamma |

**Increasing Wavelength (m)**

| $10^3$ | $10^{-2}$ | $10^{-5}$ | $5 \times 10^{-6}$ | $10^{-8}$ | $10^{-10}$ | $10^{-12}$ |
|---|---|---|---|---|---|---|

| Size of a Wavelength | Buildings | Baseball | Pinpoint | Bacteria | Viruses | Atom | Subatomic Particles |
|---|---|---|---|---|---|---|---|

You can think of light as tiny packets of electromagnetic energy called photons. Photons travel through space like waves on a pond. If photons from a distant star reach your eye, you see them as starlight. But, if those photons run into something along the way, you might not see the star at all.

What we usually think of as visible light is just a tiny slice of electromagnetic radiation, which includes low-energy radio and microwaves as well as intense and dangerous X-rays and gamma rays. To learn more about the electromagnetic spectrum, check out this video.

Crash Course light

And in the early, crowded universe, photons had plenty of things to run into. Electrons and atomic nuclei acted as roadblocks, stopping photons as soon as they started to move. Imagine trying to leave a giant, crowded party, only to keep running into trillions and trillions of people trying to say goodbye—it would take a very long time for you to get home!

For 380,000 years, nothing very exciting happened as the dark, opaque cosmos continued to expand and cool. But, once temperatures cooled to about 4,000 kelvin (6,700 degrees Fahrenheit), the fog started to lift. Atomic nuclei began snatching up electrons, pulling them into orbit to form the universe's first true hydrogen, helium, and lithium atoms.

Once these atomic roadblocks were lifted, space suddenly became transparent and the photon traffic jam cleared. A bright, brilliant flash of high-energy gamma ray photons spread through the universe, filling the cosmos with light.

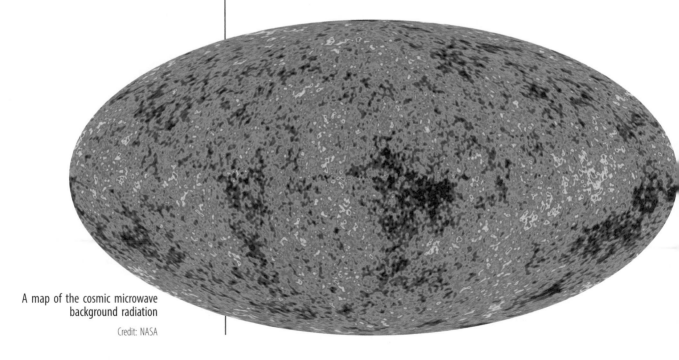

A map of the cosmic microwave background radiation

Credit: NASA

Amazingly, this first light is still detectable today as the cosmic microwave background radiation. Like a cosmic fingerprint, this cool, ancient glow is the oldest and most direct evidence of the Big Bang. As the universe continued to expand and cool, the glow slowly faded and the universe once again grew dark. With no stars to light up the cosmos, the universe entered what's called the Dark Ages. The seeds of the first stars and galaxies were beginning to form.

# THE FIRST STARS AND GALAXIES

During the Dark Ages, cosmologists think the universe was filled with a smooth, even mix of hydrogen, helium, and lithium atoms. Today, the universe still looks homogenous, or pretty much the same in all directions.

But the universe wasn't perfectly smooth and even. Slight differences in the density of space, which were incredibly small just after the Big Bang, had grown larger as the universe expanded. These small pockets of space began gathering hydrogen and helium together into little bits of matter, like clumps of clingy soap bubbles. As these clumps grew, their gravitational pull became stronger, drawing in even more matter. Very gradually, during millions of years, these clumps of atoms grew into giant clouds of swirling hydrogen and helium gas, slowly warming as they grew denser.

Around 180 million years after the Big Bang, the largest of these clouds collapsed under their own gravity, igniting their cores to become the first stars.

## COSMIC CONCEPT

About one second after the Big Bang, the observable universe was about 20 light-years across with a temperature of around 10 billion kelvin (18 billion degrees Fahrenheit).

When the first light shone across the cosmos, the observable universe was about 84 million light-years wide.

● ● ● ● ● ● ● ● ●

## SEEING THE FIRST STARS

Seeing the universe's first stars isn't easy because they are so far away. Even the Hubble Space Telescope can't pick up their dim and distant light. But new telescopes, including the James Webb Space Telescope (JWST), might be able to catch a glimpse. Set to launch in 2021, the JWST should be able to peer back far enough to see the very first stars and galaxies. This will give cosmologists a much better understanding of how the first stars and galaxies formed! You can learn more about JWST here.

🔍 NASA JWST

Astronomers aren't exactly sure when these first stars formed. Their light is too dim to detect with even the best telescopes we have today. They likely formed somewhere between 50 and 200 million years after the Big Bang. And they didn't form alone.

Huge clusters of these first stars were likely born together, and for hundreds of millions of years these brilliant star clusters collided and merged with each other to form small and lumpy protogalaxies. By the time the universe was 1 billion years old, most protogalaxies had collided and merged to form the large galaxies we see today—including the Milky Way. There was just one problem—stars and galaxies seem to have formed a little too fast.

When astronomers first measured the mass of individual galaxies, they realized that the universe did not have enough matter for stars and galaxies to form so quickly. To have enough gravitational pull, five times more matter in the universe than we can detect was needed. To make up the difference, cosmologists think some kind of strange, mysterious stuff helped pull everything together. Scientists call it dark matter.

# DARK MATTER

All "regular" matter in the universe, including stars, planets, and people, either absorbs, reflects, or emits light. For example, the sun shines, emitting light in all directions. Objects around us reflect some of this light and the retinas in our eyes absorb it—this is how we see.

But, unlike regular matter, dark matter doesn't seem to absorb, emit, or reflect any electromagnetic radiation at all.

That makes it invisible to our eyes and to any kind of telescope astronomers have used to try to detect it. The only way scientists know it's there is because of the effect its gravity has on regular matter. So, what could this massive, invisible matter be?

One possible explanation is that dark matter is just regular matter that's very hard to detect. Cosmologists call this matter massive compact halo objects (MACHOs). Large numbers of black holes, scattered around galaxies, could be a type of MACHO. Failed stars called brown dwarfs could also account for some missing matter in the universe. And although astronomers have detected a few of these dim objects, not nearly enough exist to make up all the missing matter in the universe.

## COSMIC CONCEPT

The speed of light is 670,616,629 miles per hour. It is often considered the cosmic speed limit that nothing can exceed. While nothing can move faster than light through space, the universe has no limit to how fast space itself can expand.

The South Pole Telescope during the long polar night

## VOCAB LAB

Write down what you think each word means. What root words can you find to help you? What does the context of the word tell you?

**annihilate**, **antimatter**, **cosmic inflation**, **dark matter**, **electromagnetic spectrum**, **proton**, and **quark**.

Compare your definitions with those of your friends or classmates. Did you all come up with the same meanings? Turn to the text and glossary if you need help.

## TEXT TO WORLD

What do you consider to be the most interesting moments of the Big Bang and the expansion of the universe?

Weakly interacting massive particles (WIMPs) are another possible explanation for the missing matter. WIMPs could be strange particles that have mass and exert a strong gravitational force, but barely interact with regular matter. The universe could be full of these WIMPs, zipping around and through everything, including you, without being noticed. Physicists around the world have built huge, extremely sensitive detectors hoping to catch even a single WIMP, but they haven't seen anything so far.

Whatever it is, dark matter likely formed along with regular matter not long after the Big Bang. As space expanded, dark matter would have been drawn to the denser pockets of space along with regular matter. It's extra gravitational pull would have helped draw hydrogen and helium atoms together more quickly than they could gather on their own. With this massive assist from dark matter, stars and galaxies formed in just a few million years—much sooner than they would have without the strange, invisible stuff.

Once the first stars and galaxies appeared, the universe was on its way to becoming the place we know today. For billions of years, it has continued to cool and expand, stretching out in every direction. Galaxies continue to change and evolve as new stars are born and old ones die. Let's take a closer look.

### KEY QUESTIONS

- **Why is it important to study events that happened billions of years ago?**
- **Is it difficult to think about events happening on an astronomical timescale rather than a human one?**
- **How do we know that dark matter in the universe exists if we can't see it?**

# THE EXPANDING UNIVERSE

Most cosmologists agree the universe is expanding. But it's not the stars and galaxies that are getting bigger, it's the space between them. Sound strange? Make a model of an expanding universe to get an idea of how it works!

- **Use a marker to draw five or six dots to represent galaxies on a large, uninflated balloon.** Make sure they're spread out a bit—like real galaxies in space.

- **Blow up the balloon about halfway, but don't tie off the end.** Use a clip instead. Mark one of the dots near the edge of the balloon as the Milky Way.

- **Measure the distance between the Milky Way and the other galaxies.** Record the distances. (Hint: Use a string to measure around the balloon.)

- **Fully inflate the balloon and repeat your measurements.** What happens to the "galaxies" as the balloon expands?

  - What do you notice about the distances between the Milky Way and the other galaxies?

  - How did the distance change each time you inflated the balloon?

  - Did the galaxies all travel the same distance? Why or why not?

  - Is this a good model of the expanding universe? What might be missing?

> To investigate more, try to figure out how fast the galaxies are moving. (Hint: Try measuring the time it takes to inflate the balloon.) What happens if you use a different shape of balloon? Can you think of another way to demonstrate the expansion of the universe?

# Chapter 2 ▶
# Great Galaxies

SPACE IS SO PRETTY! BUT JUST WHAT ARE WE LOOKING AT?

How do scientists use models to study events that happened long before life began?

Some things in the universe are hard to study because they are very far away or happened a long time ago. Scientists use models and simulations to understand the mysterious beginnings of objects such as galaxies!

● ● ● ● ● ● ● ● ●

**If you're lucky enough to live in a place with very dark skies, you might have noticed a faint, glowing river of light stretching overhead. With a small telescope or even a pair of binoculars, that dim glow suddenly becomes millions and millions of individual stars, packed so tightly together their distant light appears as a milky ribbon across the night sky. That glow is the Milky Way, our home galaxy.**

Today, we know that galaxies are gigantic collections of stars, planets, gas, dust, and dark matter held together by gravity. They come in lots of different shapes and sizes, from the most massive elliptical galaxies more than a million light-years across to tiny dwarf galaxies just a few hundred light-years wide. Even the smallest galaxies are home to millions of stars, while the largest can hold trillions.

It's no wonder galaxies were once called "island universes." Exactly how these huge collections of cosmic matter came together is still a bit of a mystery.

# HOW GALAXIES FORM

The formation of galaxies is one of the biggest questions in cosmology. Cosmologists think that most galaxies, including the Milky Way, started to form just a few hundred million years after the Big Bang, but just exactly when and how they formed is still a mystery. As cosmologists look back across time, galaxies appear younger, smaller, and lumpier than they do today. The youngest galaxy seen so far was already formed when the universe was just 400 million years old, so it must have been born even earlier.

Even the Hubble Space Telescope isn't powerful enough to see the birth of the first galaxies, so we haven't yet seen exactly how galaxies came to be. By using computer models and simulations, astronomers think they have an idea how galaxies such as the Milky Way might have formed.

The first galaxies likely came together not long after their most recognizable features—stars—were born. Sometime between 50 and 200 million years after the Big Bang, the first stars formed in huge clusters held together by gravity. Because everything in the universe was much closer then, these collections of stars would have collided and merged early on to form protogalaxies.

Early galaxies were probably small and lumpy, much like the youngest and most distant galaxies we can see today. The largest and fastest-growing of the early galaxies probably had a secret weapon hidden in their centers that helped them outgrow or even "eat" their neighbors—a supermassive black hole.

## COSMIC CONCEPT

The word *galaxy* comes from the Greek word *galaxias*, meaning "milky."

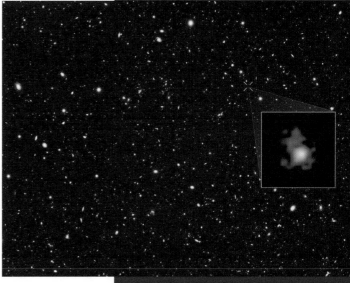

About 13.4 billion light-years away, galaxy GN-z11 is the youngest and most distant galaxy we can see. Its odd shape hints that young galaxies might have started out as small, lumpy clusters of stars.

Credit: NASA

## BLACK HOLES

### BLACK HOLES DON'T SUCK

Sometimes in movies, black holes are shown pulling in planets and spaceships to their doom. But black holes don't act like cosmic vacuums—that's not how gravity works! If the sun suddenly became a black hole today, Earth and everything else in the solar system would continue in their orbits as if nothing had changed—aside from getting cold and dark. Black holes are only dangerous if you get too close!

The active black hole at the center of M87 fires off a powerful blast of matter at nearly the speed of light.

Credit: NASA and The Hubble Heritage Team (STScI/AURA)

Black holes just might be the strangest things in the universe. Unlike their name suggests, they're not dark, empty pits in space vacuuming up everything around them. A black hole is an object that is so massive its own gravity overcomes all the other forces of nature, causing it to collapse into a tiny, dense point called a singularity.

Singularities are the dark heart of every black hole, where space, time, matter, and energy are twisted and warped and our understanding of physics breaks down. Not much is known about these bizarre objects because they're hidden behind a black hole's imaginary edge, called an event horizon. The event horizon is like an invisible point of no return.

> Anything that travels past the
> event horizon is gone forever,
> destined to fall into the singularity.
> Even light cannot escape.

While most black holes in the universe aren't much more massive than the sun, the black holes at the centers of galaxies are true monsters. They can have masses greater than millions or even billions of stars. Because they don't emit or reflect light as stars and planets do, they're dark. To find them, astronomers look to see how they affect objects nearby. When something gets too close to a black hole, such as a cloud of dust or a star, it can be torn apart and wrapped around the black hole into a quickly spinning accretion disk. As the material speeds up, friction between particles causes the disk to superheat until it glows, giving off radiation that astronomers can detect.

The first image of a black hole ever taken

Credit: European Southern Observatory (ESO)
(CC BY International 4.0)

Today, most supermassive black holes in older galaxies such as the Milky Way are dark and quiet, occasionally sipping on a passing gas cloud or munching on an unlucky star. This can make them very hard to detect. But, in younger galaxies with very bright centers called active galactic nuclei (AGN), black holes are much easier to spot. Given a large supply of dust and gas, these supermassive black holes will pull tremendous amounts of material into their accretion disks, where it's compressed and heated to millions of degrees.

Some of this matter gets pushed to the black hole's magnetic poles, where it's blasted into space as powerful jets of radiation. If these jets happen to be pointed in the direction of Earth, they appear as quasars, some of the brightest and most powerful objects in the universe. A quasar, which is short for "quasi-stellar radio source," is so powerful it can outshine all the stars in its galaxy.

## SAY CHEESE!

The snapshot of the supermassive black hole at the center of the M87 galaxy was years in the making. Astronomers pieced together radio wave images taken during a decade that show hot, glowing gas as it circles the black hole's event horizon. To learn more about the image and what it took to make it, read the article at this website. How long did it take for scientists to take the picture and why? What parts of the black hole can you see and what is hidden? Will there be other pictures of black holes in the future? Before astronomers knew what the first picture of a black hole would show, they used computer simulations to predict what they'd see. How can simulations of objects help scientists understand them better? How does the predicted picture match up with the final image? Why do you think they're different?

🔍 JPL NASA first image

Galaxy NGC 2623, formed by the violent collision of two galaxies

Credit: NASA/ESA Hubble Space Telescope

As galaxies continued to grow and evolve, many collided with each other in spectacular cosmic pileups. Although these collisions were more common in the past, they are still happening today.

Even the Milky Way and the Andromeda Galaxy are headed for a crash—in about 4.5 billion years!

Galaxies have continued to evolve for billions of years, shaped by collisions and mergers to become the huge collections of stars, gas, and dust we see today.

Just like people, no two galaxies are alike. Some look like round, fuzzy patches of light, while some appear twisted into amazing pinwheel shapes. Others look like they've been torn apart, with no real shape at all. Astronomers classify galaxies using the Hubble tuning fork diagram, which sorts them into three basic shapes: spiral, elliptical, and irregular.

In the early universe, galaxies often collided and merged with each other to form even larger galaxies. Check out these supercomputer simulations of galaxies merging!

 NASA visualization galaxy

# SPIRAL GALAXIES

With their winding, pinwheel-like spiral arms, it's easy to see why these majestic collections of stars are called spiral galaxies. Spiral galaxies are everywhere and seem to make up about two-thirds of all galaxies in the universe, including our own Milky Way. Spiral galaxies come in lots of different sizes, from small galaxies tens of thousands of light-years across to giants stretching more than 500,000 light-years wide. No matter their size, all spiral galaxies have a few things in common.

Spiral galaxies are flat, pancake-like disks of gas, dust, and stars surrounding a bright central bulge, or nucleus. The nucleus is a tightly packed sphere of mostly older, redder stars usually surrounding a supermassive black hole.

Twisting out and away from the nucleus are the magnificent spiral arms that give spiral galaxies their shape and name. Most of a spiral galaxy's gas and dust can be found in its spiral arms, where they collapse to form younger, bluer stars. The clouds of star-making material can also create dark and dramatic dust lanes in some galaxies, appearing as inky-black bands that block the light of the stars behind them.

> Astronomers aren't sure how spiral galaxies get their unique shape.

One possible explanation is a density wave, which is like a traffic jam made of gas and dust. As clouds of interstellar material collapse, their movement sends waves through the galaxy's disk. As the waves run into other clouds, they bunch together and collapse, forming new stars along a winding, spiral path.

The sun and the rest of the solar system are located about 26,000 light years from the center of the Milky Way in the Orion Spur, a small, quiet branch of the giant Sagittarius spiral arm. Check out other regions of the Milky Way in this chart!

 NASA charting Milky Way

The Sombrero Galaxy, or M104, is an Sa-type galaxy that appears almost edge-on to us, making its tightly wound spiral arms a little difficult to see. About half the size of the Milky Way and roughly 50,000 light-years away, it's known for the very large dust lane on its outer edge.

Credit: NASA, ESA, and The Hubble Heritage Team (STScI/AURA)

NGC 1300, a barred spiral galaxy with loosely wound arms, is an example of an SBb galaxy. About 110,000 light-years across, NGC 1300 is nearly the same size as the Milky Way and is about 61 million light-years away in the constellation Eridanus.

Credit: NASA, ESA, and The Hubble Heritage Team (STScI/AURA)

M51, known as the Whirlpool Galaxy, is an example of an Sc-type galaxy and was the first galaxy classified as a spiral galaxy. A little smaller than the Milky Way, the Whirlpool Galaxy is about 23 million light-years distant and has a smaller companion galaxy on the upper right.

Credit: NASA and ESA

Some spiral galaxies also have a bright line or bar running through their nucleus, with spiral arms unwrapping from the ends. These barred spirals make up about half of all spiral galaxies, and astronomers think the Milky Way is one of them.

When astronomers classify spiral galaxies, they label them with a capital S for spiral and Sb for barred spiral. They also use lowercase letters to describe how tightly wound the spiral arms appear. Sa galaxies have very tight and compact spiral arms, while Sc galaxies are looser and more open.

# ELLIPTICAL GALAXIES

Elliptical galaxies are some of biggest galaxies in the universe, with the largest spanning millions of light years and containing trillions of stars. Like spiral galaxies, elliptical galaxies usually have a bright central bulge hiding a supermassive black hole, but that's where their similarities end.

> Elliptical galaxies lack the beautiful twisting arms of spiral galaxies.

Instead of circling the galactic center in a flat disk, the stars in elliptical galaxies orbit at random angles, giving them a fuzzy, football-like appearance. Elliptical galaxies are also missing most of the interstellar gas and dust of spiral galaxies. Instead, they're filled with mostly ancient, red stars that formed long ago. Astronomers think elliptical galaxies form when spiral galaxies collide and merge, causing them to use up most of their gas and dust in a huge burst of star formation, wiping away their old spiral arms.

## COSMIC CONCEPT

The largest known galaxy is thought to be galaxy IC 1101. It's estimated to be more than 6 million light-years across, more than 60 times wider than the Milky Way. It may hold as many as 100 trillion stars!

With billions and billions of galaxies in the universe, it's hard for astronomers to analyze and classify every single one. But you can help! As a citizen scientist at zooniverse.org, you can help real astronomers discover and classify new galaxies around the universe. To participate check out this website.

 zooniverse galaxy zoo

The large, fuzzy object in the picture is M60, an E1 elliptical galaxy. Next to it is NGC 4647, a dramatic spiral galaxy. Astronomers think these two galaxies, each about 60 million light-years away, are close enough for both to feel the effects of the other's gravity.

Credit: NASA, ESA, and The Hubble Heritage Team (STScI/AURA)-ESA/Hubble Collaboration

M59 is an E5 elliptical galaxy about 48 million light-years away. At around 76,000 light-years across, it's smaller than the Milky Way and contains mostly old, red stars.

Credit: ESA/Hubble & NASA, P. Cote

NGC 4866 is a lenticular galaxy about 80 million light-years from Earth. It appears almost edge-on to us, and although it doesn't have spiral arms, it does have some dark clouds of dust and a bright nucleus.

Because elliptical galaxies don't have spiral arms, they're a little easier to classify. On the Hubble tuning fork diagram, ellipticals are given the classification E for elliptical, followed by a number from 0 to 7. A galaxy classified as E0 would face directly at us and look almost perfectly round, while a galaxy classified as E7 would be edge-on to us and appear as a very long, thin ellipse.

If astronomers have trouble deciding if a galaxy is an elliptical or spiral galaxy, it might be a lenticular galaxy. Lenticular galaxies seem to fit somewhere in between. Like spiral galaxies, lenticular galaxies have a large central bulge surrounded by a wide, flat disk. Like elliptical galaxies, they don't have spiral arms or much gas and dust. Lenticular galaxies are classified as SO on the Hubble tuning fork diagram.

# IRREGULAR GALAXIES

The universe has many spiral and elliptical galaxies, but lots of galaxies don't fit in with either crowd. These lumpy, misshapen collections of stars are called irregular galaxies. Instead of being fuzzy ellipses or having pinwheeling arms, most irregular galaxies don't have a regular shape or a bright nucleus. They're usually smaller than their elliptical or spiral cousins and have lots of gas and dust.

With all this star-making material available, most irregular galaxies are filled with hot, young stars that make them very bright. You will learn about how stars are formed in the next chapter.

## COSMIC CONCEPT

The Milky Way has a mass of about 1.5 trillion suns.

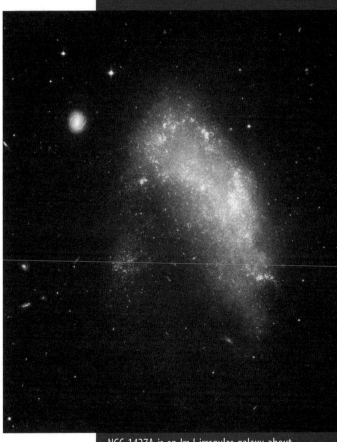

NGC 1427A is an Irr-I irregular galaxy about 52 million light-years away. Just 20,000 light-years across, it's much smaller than the Milky Way and has no spiral arms or bright nucleus. The spiral galaxy to its left is 25 times farther away.

Credit: NASA, ESA, and The Hubble Heritage Team (STScI/AURA)

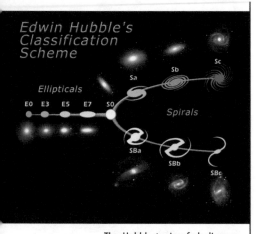

*Edwin Hubble's Classification Scheme*

The Hubble tuning fork diagram

Credit: NASA & ESA

Irregular galaxies are classified as either type Irr-I or Irr-II. Irr-I galaxies have a little structure to them, maybe a hint of spiral arms or a nucleus, while Irr-II galaxies have no structure at all.

Some irregular galaxies might be pieces of larger galaxies, torn away or knocked free in collisions with other galaxies. Many irregular galaxies orbit larger spiral and elliptical galaxies, including the Milky Way. The Large Magellanic Cloud and the Small Magellanic Cloud are just two of the Milky Way's galactic companions, circling our galaxy about 160,000 to 200,000 light-years away. They may have been captured or torn apart by the Milky Way at some point in the past.

A X-ray view of the Milky Way from the Chandra X-ray Observatory. The center of the Milky Way is the bright area in the upper left, which hides a supermassive black hole called Sagittarius A*!

Credit: NASA/JPL-Caltech/ESA/CXC/STScI

# YOU ARE HERE

The Milky Way is our home galaxy, the one we know best. It formed not long after the Big Bang, about 13 to 14 billion years ago, and has been evolving ever since. Because we're inside it, it's hard to know what the Milky Way looks like, but if we could peer down on its spiral arms and bright nucleus from above, we'd see a large, barred spiral galaxy.

The Milky Way is home to somewhere between 100 and 400 billion stars. It stretches about 100,000 light-years from edge to edge and is just 1,000 light-years thick in the disk, which is where its spiral arms are found. The spiral arms are filled with clouds of gas,

dust, and young stars—including the sun. Our solar system is located in the Orion Spur, a small branch of the Sagittarius arm about 26,000 light years from the galactic center.

> Our part of the Milky Way is like a quiet suburb of a large city.

Things get much busier toward the galaxy's nucleus. There, gas, dust, and hundreds of millions of older stars are packed so tightly together that they hide the true heart of the Milky Way—a supermassive black hole named Sagittarius A* (pronounced Sagittarius A-star).

## COSMIC CONCEPT

As the solar system orbits the Milky Way, it's moving about 515,000 miles per hour—around 300 times faster than a bullet. But even at this speed, it takes about 225 million years to complete one galactic orbit.

## A MYSTERIOUS PULL

In the 1960s, astronomer Vera Rubin (1928–2016) discovered something strange about galaxies. In our solar system, planets closer to the sun move faster in their orbits than planets farther out. But in galaxies, stars circling at the outer edge move just as fast as those near the galactic center. Rubin realized that some hidden matter must be tugging on these outer stars, and her discovery became the first direct evidence for dark matter. Astronomers now believe most galaxies are surrounded by a halo of invisible dark matter. To learn more about Vera Rubin's important discovery, check out this video.

🔍 SciShow Vera Rubin

With a mass 4 million times greater than the sun packed into a space 14.6 million miles wide, Sagittarius A* is a true monster of a black hole. Although it can't be seen directly, astronomers have detected radio waves and X-rays coming from its super-hot accretion disk, which flares up whenever material gets too close.

Outside the Milky Way is the galactic halo, an approximately 600,000 light-year-wide sphere of gas, old stars, and dark matter that surrounds the entire galaxy. Scattered throughout the halo are groups of ancient stars called globular clusters. These spherical collections of stars probably formed when the galaxy was very young and have been circling it ever since.

> Despite its supermassive black hole and hundreds of billions of stars, most of the Milky Way's mass seems to be hidden in the galactic halo as dark matter.

With its added gravitational pull, dark matter helps stars in the outer edges of the galaxy rotate almost as fast as those close to the center.

## OUR GALACTIC NEIGHBORHOOD

Even though they're separated by great distances, most galaxies aren't cosmic loners. They tend to hang together in groups and clusters, forming some of the largest structures in the universe. Even the Milky Way is part of a collection of galaxies called the Local Group. The Local Group spans about 10 million light years and contains around 50 galaxies, the largest being the Andromeda, Milky Way, and Triangulum galaxies.

Each of these larger galaxies is surrounded by several satellite galaxies—the Milky Way has at least 13. The rest of the members in the group are mostly small and irregular dwarf galaxies drifting around and between the big three.

> The Local Group might seem big, but it's just a small part of the much larger Virgo Cluster, a huge collection of more than 1,000 large and small galaxies spanning an incredible 65 million light years.

And the Virgo Cluster is one part of a giant collection of galaxies in the enormous Laniakea Supercluster. With 100,000 galaxies of every shape and size reaching 520 million light years in diameter, the Laniakea Supercluster is still just one of 10 million superclusters in the entire observable universe!

No matter where we point a telescope, we find galaxies of all shapes and sizes. Astronomers think that the entire observable universe may include as many as 2 trillion galaxies! Galaxies are truly gigantic, incredible objects. But, without stars, galaxies would not exist.

## KEY QUESTIONS

- **How are black holes different in real life from how they are depicted in science fiction?**
- **What challenges do astronomers and cosmologists face when studying galaxies?**

## VOCAB LAB

Write down what you think each word means. What root words can you find to help you? What does the context of the word tell you?

**barred spiral**, **black hole**, **elliptical galaxy**, **event horizon**, **galactic halo**, **interstellar**, **quasar**, and **singularity**.

Compare your definitions with those of your friends or classmates. Did you all come up with the same meanings? Turn to the text and glossary if you need help.

## TEXT TO WORLD

The Milky Way isn't the only galaxy you can see without a telescope! You can catch the faint glow of the massive Andromeda galaxy under very dark skies!

# MODEL THE MILKY WAY

From inside the Milky Way, it's hard to understand its size and shape. But, thanks to the careful measurement of thousands of stars, astronomers have a pretty good idea what the Milky Way would look like if we could see it from the outside. Try constructing a model of the Milky Way.

- **Research the Milky Way to understand how to create your model.**

- **Choose any materials and medium you want to make your model.** Make sure you represent the Milky Way's disk, bulge, and spiral arms.

- **Consider these questions as you design your model.**

  - Will the model be two- or three-dimensional?

  - Will it be a physical or computer model?

  - How detailed will you make the model and how will you label it?

  - Will you accurately represent the scale of the Milky Way's disc, bulge, and spiral arms?

  - The Milky Way has several satellite galaxies, including the Large and Small Magellanic Clouds. Can you represent them in your model? What would be the correct size and distance?

- **Assemble your model and adjust it as needed.** Use your model to explain to a friend or classmate the structure of the Milky Way.

To investigate more, consider that astronomers think the Milky Way might be warped like a bent frisbee! How could that affect your model? What would you do differently? Check out this website for more information on the bent frisbee theory!

🔍 PBS galaxy warped

# Chapter 3
# Stellar Stars

HAVE YOU HEARD THE QUOTE, "WE ARE MADE OF STAR STUFF"?

CARL SAGAN SAID THAT!

Why do stars play a large role in cultural stories?

People have always used stories to explain things we can't understand. Through this tradition, human groups throughout time and place have developed narratives that feature stars, which have always sparkled above us.

● ● ● ● ● ● ● ● ●

**Have you ever been stargazing? Depending on where you live, you can see dozens, hundreds, or even thousands of stars shining in the night sky. For centuries, people of different cultures have looked to the stars as calendars marking the passing of time, as shapes to honor myths and legends, and as a guide to help explorers navigate Earth.**

Today, we know that stars are gigantic spheres of super-hot plasma, made of mostly hydrogen and helium gas and held together by their own gravity. They're powered by nuclear fusion, an atomic reaction deep within their cores that provides all the energy they need to shine.

Plus, stars forge in their deaths all the elements heavier than hydrogen and helium, seeding the universe with the ingredients for new stars, planets, and even life. Without stars, there would be no oxygen to breathe, no water to drink, and no Earth beneath our feet.

# A STAR IS BORN

All stars begin their lives the same way—as tiny bits of matter in a vast, cold cloud of interstellar gas and dust called a nebula. Made mostly of hydrogen and helium, nebulas can drift quietly in the space between stars for millions of years. But, if a nebula is stirred up, maybe by the explosion of a nearby star or even a passing asteroid or comet, interesting things can happen. Molecules of gas and dust begin to bump together and stick, at first forming small clumps of matter no bigger than a grain of sand. These tiny grains are the seeds of stars.

As the clumps get larger, their gravitational pull increases, gathering even more material and gradually forming a giant, swirling cloud of dust and gas. As it grows, gravity squeezes the center of the cloud tighter and tighter, forming a hot and dense core. As it heats up, the rest of the cloud is stretched out into a spinning, pancake-like shape, called an accretion disk, around the core. It's from this disk that planets can form.

When temperatures inside the core reach about 1,500 kelvin (2,240 degrees Fahrenheit), the massive cloud becomes a glowing protostar. But a protostar isn't a star—not yet. Its core has to reach the searing temperatures needed to start nuclear fusion.

Fusion is what separates stars from everything else in the universe. Under tremendous pressures and temperatures, atoms of hydrogen smash together with such force that they fuse, or combine, to make helium atoms. This releases an incredible amount of energy in the form of photons, which create all of a star's light and heat. These photons push back against the star's crushing gravity, keeping it from collapsing. When they make it to the surface and stream off into space, we have starlight.

Many cultures mentally arranged the stars in the night sky into shapes and patterns, often representing characters from myths and legends. The 88 constellations we have mostly include ancient Greek heroes such as Orion the hunter and animals such as Leo the lion—along with some less mythical things, including Telescopium the telescope. You can explore the night sky and the constellations here!

 star atlas

## COSMIC CONCEPT

"The nitrogen in our DNA, the calcium in our teeth, the iron in our blood, the carbon in our apple pies were made in the interiors of collapsing stars. We are made of star stuff."

—Carl Sagan (1934–1996), American astronomer

## SIBLING STARS

Not all stars are loners like the sun. Stars often form in pairs called binary star systems. The nearest star system to our own, Alpha Centauri, is a triple star system. It has two sun-like stars named Alpha Centauri A and Alpha Centauri B, which are both orbited by a faint and distant red dwarf—a small and relatively cool star—called Proxima Centauri, the closest star to Earth at just 4.22 light-years away. Proxima even has an Earth-sized exoplanet! You can learn more about the Alpha Centauri star system at this website.

Space Alpha Centauri

To achieve fusion and become a star, a protostar needs to have at least 8 percent of the sun's mass. If it doesn't, it'll fizzle out and become a brown dwarf, a failed star that never shines. But, if the protostar grows large enough, gravity will keep squeezing the core tighter and raising its temperature. Once it reaches 10 million kelvin (17,999,540 degrees Fahrenheit), the core will ignite—a new star is born.

# CLASSIFYING STARS

Once fusion begins, a star leaves its childhood behind to become an adult, or main sequence star. Stars spend most of their lives on the main sequence, shining steadily for as long as they have hydrogen fuel in their cores. How long that fuel lasts depends on a star's mass.

Nearly all the characteristics of a main sequence star—color, temperature, lifespan—depend on its mass. The biggest and hottest main sequence stars, blue supergiants, can be hundreds of times more massive than the sun and shine a million times brighter. That mass means big stars live fast and die young, sprinting furiously through their nuclear fuel in just a few million years. Because their lives are so short, these giant stars are rare.

> The smallest stars, cool and dim red dwarfs, are the ultra-marathon runners of the stellar family.

With less than half the mass of the sun, these cool stars sip at their hydrogen fuel and will still be shining trillions of years in the future, long after larger stars have burned out. Red dwarfs are the most common type of stars, making up 75 percent of all stars in the universe.

| Spectral Type | Color | Surface Temperature (kelvin) | Example Stars |
|---|---|---|---|
| O | Blue | 30,000 K or more | Alnitak, Zeta Ophiuchi |
| B | Blue-white | 10,000–30,000 K | Rigel, Regulus |
| A | White | 7,500–10,000 K | Sirius, Vega |
| F | Yellow-white | 6,000–7,500 K | Canopus, Procyon A |
| G | Yellow | 5,500–6,000 K | Sun, Alpha Centauri, Tau Ceti |
| K | Orange | 3,500–5,000 K | Arcturus, Pollux |
| M | Red | 2,000–3,500 K | Betelgeuse, Proxima Centauri |

However, you wouldn't know it looking at the night sky. Red dwarfs are too dim to be seen with the naked eye, making most stars in the universe invisible without a telescope!

While mass is a star's most important characteristic, measuring the mass of a star from light-years away isn't easy. Instead, astronomers classify main sequence stars according to their color and temperature. Have you ever seen something glow white-hot? When you heat a piece of metal it begins to change color, from red to orange to white. And, if it doesn't melt, it will eventually glow a searing blueish white!

Like glowing hot metal, a star's color is related to its surface temperature. Astronomers use a spectrograph to analyze a star's light, carefully measuring color and temperature to determine its spectral type.

Fusion is an amazing and complex atomic process, one that produces enough energy to keep the sun shining for billions of years. Physicists and engineers on Earth have tried for decades to harness the power of the sun by building fusion reactors here on Earth. Could fusion solve the world's energy problems? Learn more about fusion power in this video.

🔍 Kurzgesagt fusion power

## TWINKLE, TWINKLE, LITTLE STAR

The twinkling of a star doesn't come from the stars themselves but from Earth's atmosphere. As starlight travels through the atmosphere, changes in temperature, pressure, and even wind can slightly bend the light's path on its way to your eye. It's this atmospheric turbulence that makes stars appear to twinkle!

COSMIC CONCEPT

Does that star look different to you? Most stars, including the sun, go through small changes in their brightness. But some stars change brightness dramatically! Betelgeuse, a red supergiant and usually the 10th brightest star in the sky, dimmed so much in early 2020 that it became just the 21st brightest star in the sky! Variable stars often grow brighter and dimmer on a regular schedule, or period. How bright is Betelgeuse today?

## HOW OLD ARE YOU?

How do we know the age of the sun? Scientists examine the oldest things they can find in the solar system—ancient rocks. By examining samples from meteorites, the moon, and Earth, we've learned that the most ancient rocks all formed around 4.5 billion years ago. By comparing how quickly the sun uses its fuel to the age of these oldest rocks, we find the ages match!

With surface temperatures of 30,000 kelvin (53,540 degrees Fahrenheit) or higher, the hottest blue supergiants are classified as O-type stars. The smallest and dimmest red dwarfs have surface temperatures between 2,000 and 3,500 kelvin (3,140 to 5,840 degrees Fahrenheit) and are classified as M-type stars.

Because each spectral type has a range of temperatures, the numbers 0 through 9 are used to classify stars in more detail. For example, Sirius has a temperature of about 9,900 kelvin (17,360 degrees Fahrenheit) and is an A1 star, while cooler Vega, with a temperature of around 9,600 kelvin (16,820 degrees Fahrenheit) is classified as an A0 star.

A typical star will spend billions of years as a main sequence star. Fortunately, we have one nearby.

The sun might not be the biggest or brightest star in the universe, but it gives us an up-close look at how an average star lives and works.

# A MIDDLE-AGED STAR: THE SUN

Just 93 million miles from Earth, the sun brightens our days, holds the planets in their orbits, and is the main source of energy for nearly all life on Earth. But while it's special to us, to a distant alien astronomer, the sun would be just another star.

With a surface temperature of 5,780 kelvin (9,944 degrees Fahrenheit) the sun is a main sequence yellow dwarf star, one of millions just like it in the Milky Way. It formed along with the rest of the solar system about 4.5 billion years ago from a collapsing cloud of dust and gas and has been shining steadily ever since.

Deep within the sun lies the source of all its energy—a massive, 200,000-mile-wide, fusion-powered furnace called the core. Crushed by the sun's tremendous gravitational force, the core is an amazingly hot and dense place, with a temperature of about 15 million kelvin (27 million degrees Fahrenheit) and a pressure 250 billion times greater than what we feel on Earth.

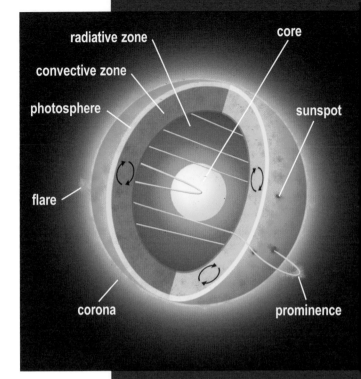

Every second, 700 million tons of hydrogen are fused into helium, while about 5 million tons are converted directly into energy in the form of gamma ray photons. These high-energy photons carry the core's energy outward into the radiative zone, a crowded, cooler layer surrounding the core. In the radiative zone, energy from the core travels slowly, atom by atom, until it reaches the convective zone.

In the convective zone, the sun's energy travels by convection, like bubbles in a boiling pot of soup. Giant blobs of super-hot plasma heated from below cool as they rise toward the sun's surface, or photosphere, where they stream out into space as sunlight. By the time the photons from the core reach the photosphere, their temperature has dropped from millions of degrees to just 5,780 kelvin (9,944 degrees Fahrenheit)—much cooler than the core, but still hot enough to melt diamonds!

Beyond the photosphere is the sun's strange, hot atmosphere. First is the chromosphere, a thin layer of mostly hydrogen gas that's five times hotter than the surface below. But that's nothing compared to the heat of the mysterious corona.

## A Photon's Journey

A photon leaving the surface of the sun takes about eight minutes and 20 seconds to travel the 93 million miles to Earth. But it takes about 170,000 years for a photon to travel the much shorter 432,000 miles from the sun's core to its surface! The interior of the sun is so crowded that photons can't travel in a straight line. Instead, they're scattered in all directions, making their way out blindly in what scientists call a „random walk."

The corona's wispy tendrils stream away from the sun for millions of miles, reaching temperatures of 1 million kelvin (1,800,000 degrees Fahrenheit). To see the elusive corona, you need to dial down the brightness of the entire sun. On Earth, that only happens during a solar eclipse, when the moon passes directly between the sun and Earth. **NEVER LOOK DIRECTLY AT THE SUN WITHOUT PROPER PROTECTION**, even during a solar eclipse. It can cause permanent damage to your eyes!

> Solar physicists aren't sure what gives the sun's atmosphere its intense heat, but they think it might be related to the sun's powerful magnetic field.

Although it's hard to tell from Earth, the sun's surface can be a very active place. Much of the sun's activity comes from deep beneath the surface, where electrically charged plasma creates the sun's incredibly strong magnetic field. As the sun turns on its axis, the magnetic field twists, bends, and breaks, causing planet-sized blemishes and violent eruptions.

Dark, cooler, planet-sized blotches called sunspots often mark the sun's surface. These sunspots are sometimes accompanied by intense blasts of radiation called solar flares, which take place when the sun's magnetic field tangles and breaks. The sun's magnetic field can also pull and twist hot plasma into giant, fiery loops called solar prominences.

The largest and most powerful solar events, however, are coronal mass ejections (CMEs). CMEs are gigantic bubbles of hot plasma and radiation that explode from the sun's surface and can travel through the solar system with tremendous speed. If they reach Earth, CMEs can damage satellites, disrupt communications, and even cause power outages.

You can see the sun's corona during a solar eclipse. Never look directly at the sun!

Credit: NASA's Goddard Space Flight Center/Gopalswamy

## COSMIC CONCEPT

The sun isn't a particularly big or small star, but with a diameter of 860,000 miles, it's so large that about 1.3 million Earths could fit inside it. The sun is 300,000 times more massive than Earth and makes up 99.8 percent of all the mass in our solar system.

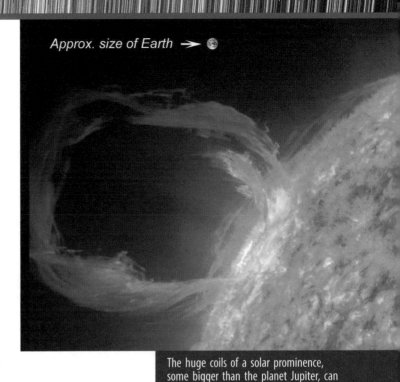

*Approx. size of Earth* ➜ 🌑

Similar to seasons on Earth, the sun's activity follows a mostly predictable 11-year schedule called the solar cycle. At the peak, or solar maximum, the sun may have dozens of sunspots along with lots of flares and CMEs. During the solar minimum, months or even years may pass without a sunspot or burp of plasma.

For more than 4 billion years, the sun has led a remarkably steady life. But, like all stars, it must eventually come to an end.

The huge coils of a solar prominence, some bigger than the planet Jupiter, can last several months before casting their plasma out into space.

## HOW STARS DIE

While stars can live for millions, billions, and even trillions of years, they can't last forever. All stars will eventually run out of hydrogen fuel and leave the main sequence behind. For the smallest stars, the end of their lives will happen very slowly during trillions of years as they gradually run out of fuel.

The largest stars flame out in just a few million years, their deaths leaving behind some of the most bizarre objects in the universe. But, for an average-sized star such as the sun, death is somewhere in between.

It's hard to imagine the end of the sun, but it's coming. The sun is about halfway through its main sequence of about 9 billion years.

Check out this video of sunspots on the surface of the sun. What other features can you spot?

🔍 Goddard two sunspot

**STELLAR STARS** 51

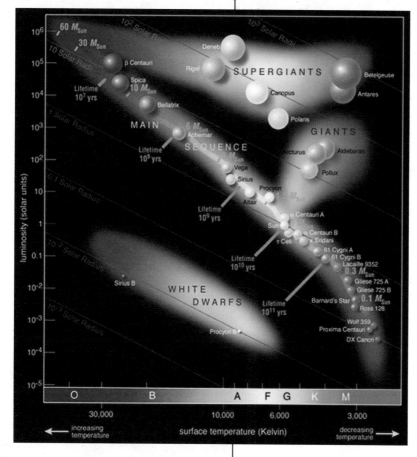

Astronomers use the Hertzsprung-Russel (or H-R) diagram to show how a star's luminosity, color, and temperature are related during a star's life cycle. When stars use up the last of their hydrogen fuel, they leave the main sequence behind.

Credit: ESO (CC BY 4.0 International)

About 5.4 billion years from now, the sun will use the last of the hydrogen fuel in its core and nuclear fusion will stop. Without the steady pressure of photons, gravity will cause the outer layers of the sun to collapse onto the core of helium. This crash will start a new round of hydrogen fusion in a shell around the burned-out core, expanding the sun to 100 times its current size. When this happens, the sun will no longer be a main sequence star. It will become a hugely swollen stellar monster called a red giant.

As the hydrogen fusion shell keeps burning, the helium core underneath will be squeezed tighter and tighter until it reignites, fusing helium to make carbon and oxygen. But, with nowhere to go, the energy in the core will quickly build until it explodes in a helium flash, releasing more energy than today's sun could put out in 200 million years. You might think this tremendous explosion would destroy the sun, but the blast of energy will fuse half the core's helium into carbon. This will actually cause the sun to shrink!

The Parker Solar Probe, launched in 2018, is the first spacecraft to "touch" the sun by flying through its corona. Scientists hope to learn a lot more about the sun, including how and why its atmosphere is so much hotter than its surface. You can follow the mission at this website.

 NASA Parker probe

For a few hundred million years, the sun will keep fusing hydrogen and helium, expanding and contracting as the last of its fuel runs out. As its twin fusion engines sputter, the dying star will gradually cast off its outer layers into space to form a planetary nebula.

When fusion stops for good, the last of our sun's outer layers will collapse a final time, heating the core before being tossed off into space. In the end, only the white-hot core will be left behind. This final remnant of the sun, about the diameter of Earth, is called a white dwarf. No longer producing energy, the white dwarf will gradually fade during several trillion years until it becomes the same cold temperature as space itself. All that will remain is a dark, frigid cinder called a black dwarf.

Our sun won't be alone in its cold death. Most stars that are the sun's size or smaller will eventually become black dwarfs. Only the most massive stars avoid this fate—and their deaths are some of the strangest and most spectacular events in the cosmos.

## SUPERNOVAS AND MORE

For medium-sized stars such as the sun, fusing helium into carbon and oxygen is their last desperate attempt to keep going. But for stars with more than eight times the mass of the sun, fusion doesn't end with helium. These big stars can keep fusing heavier and heavier atoms until they form iron.

Fusing iron into larger atoms takes a star more energy than it releases, and when a massive star's core is full of iron, all fusion stops. In less than a second, the giant star will collapse with tremendous force, bouncing off the core in a violent explosion called a supernova.

The sun as a red giant (diameter ≈ 2 AU)

The sun as a main-sequence star (diameter ≈ 0.01 AU)

AU stands for an astronomical unit (AU). One AU is the distance from the sun to Earth.

One of the earliest known supernovas was recorded by Chinese and Korean astronomers in 1054 BCE. Appearing as a dazzling new star, it shined in the sky for two years and was so bright it was visible during the day. Today, its remains are the beautiful Crab Nebula.

Credit: NASA, ESA, J. Hester, A. Loll (ASU)

## COSMIC CONCEPT

Supernovas are super rare! In a galaxy the size of the Milky Way, they happen only about once every 50 years.

Supernovas are some of the most powerful explosions in the universe. They can briefly outshine entire galaxies and put out more energy than the sun will release during its entire life. What's left behind after a supernova might be even more amazing. The explosion is so powerful that the core, slightly more massive than the sun, is crushed to the size of a small city. Under such tremendous pressure, protons and electrons are mashed together to form neutrons. All that's left is a 12.5-mile wide, rapidly spinning ball of neutrons called a neutron star.

Neutron stars also have very strong magnetic fields that shoot powerful beams of electromagnetic energy from their poles. As they spin, these beams of radiation sweep through space, and if they happen to cross our path, they're detected as short pulses of radio waves. Astronomers call these pulsars. The fastest pulsars spin more than 600 times a second.

Similar to white dwarfs, neutron stars will eventually cool off to become cold, dark husks. The largest stars in the universe have an even stranger fate. For stars with a mass more than 20 times greater than that of the sun, their end is the beginning of the most mysterious object in the universe—a stellar black hole. When a giant star explodes, the gravitational force squeezing the core is so strong that nothing can stop its collapse. The entire core collapses on itself, disappearing behind the event horizon of a stellar black hole.

Stellar black holes are just like the supermassive black holes at the center of galaxies, only smaller. These star-sized black holes are much harder to detect. Astronomers estimate the Milky Way could have between 10 million and 1 billion stellar black holes, quietly and darkly moving through space. To find them, astronomers look for the effect they have on objects that circle them, such as companion stars.

## LONG LIVE THE RED DWARFS!

For the smallest red dwarf stars, death comes slowly. After trillions of years on the main sequence, they'll eventually run out of hydrogen fuel. But, instead of ballooning into red giants, they'll simply become white dwarfs and eventually fade until they become black dwarfs. Because the universe has only been around a few billion years, no red dwarf shining today is even close to dying a natural death.

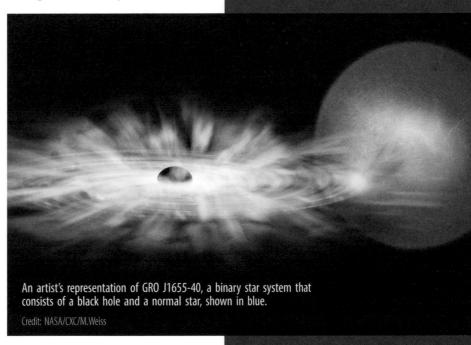

An artist's representation of GRO J1655-40, a binary star system that consists of a black hole and a normal star, shown in blue.

Credit: NASA/CXC/M.Weiss

Pulsars are some of the strangest objects in the universe. Their very fast and regular pulses are more accurate than the best stopwatch. To learn more about them, check out this video from NASA.

🔍 NASA pulsar video

One of the first objects suspected to be a stellar black hole, Cygnus X-1, is circled by a large, blue companion star. Astronomers believe that the black hole pulls material off the nearby star, drawing it into a swirling accretion disk. As the material falls toward Cygnus X-1, it heats up, creating powerful X-ray jets that are detectable on Earth.

As spectacularly strange as black holes and neutron stars are, their formation isn't the most important thing to come from the death of large stars. The death of stars also makes planets such as Earth possible.

Nearly all the elements in the universe that are not hydrogen and helium are created in the hearts of dead and dying stars. During the final second of a massive star's life, the heat and pressure of a supernova is enough to forge very small amounts of heavier elements such as iron, oxygen, carbon, and gold—the building blocks of planets and life as we know it.

The sun and our entire solar system formed from the remnants of long dead stars, their deaths having resulted in asteroids, comets, moons, and planets—and even life on Earth.

## TEXT TO WORLD

How might humans use fusion to help with energy issues here on Earth?

**KEY QUESTIONS**

- **Why is it accurate to say that everything we know is the stuff of stars?**
- **Do you think humans should be trying to find ways of keeping our sun from dying?**
- **Why do scientists use color and temperature to classify stars?**

# BIG STARS, LITTLE STARS, AND THE SUN

Nuclear fusion may cause all stars to shine, but that doesn't mean all stars are the same. Some are much smaller than the sun, while others are much, much larger!

- **How would you create a scale model to compare the sun to another star?** Research an interesting star to compare to the sun. Will it be a nearby star? One you can see in the sky? A giant or a dwarf?

- **How will you make your models?** Use any materials you like—paint, paper, pencil, sculpting, 3-D printing. Or start with something simple you have at home, such as a marble or a soccer ball!

- **When making an accurate model, the scale factor is important.** For example, the sun's diameter is 109 times Earth's diameter. If you made a 1-inch model of Earth, the sun would need to be 109 inches across to be to scale. Choose your scale carefully to make your model as accurate as possible!

> To investigate more, consider how far your star is from the sun. How could you build a scale model to represent the distance? What stars are the sun's closest relatives?

## VOCAB LAB

Write down what you think each word means. What root words can you find to help you? What does the context of the word tell you?

**convective zone**, **corona**, **nebula**, **main sequence star**, **protostar**, **pulsar**, **solar flare**, **stellar black hole**, and **supernova**.

Compare your definitions with those of your friends or classmates. Did you all come up with the same meanings? Turn to the text and glossary if you need help.

# BUILD A SUNSPOT SPOTTER

The surface of the sun is a hot, active place, but sunspots are (relatively) cool! You can build your own sunspot viewer to track and view sunspots as they turn with the sun.

**Be careful—never look directly at the sun. Viewing the sun directly can permanently damage your eyes!**

## Ideas for Supplies ▼

- aluminum foil
- tack, pin, or needle
- small cardboard box about 2 to 3 feet long
- sheet of white paper

- **Gather your supplies and follow these steps to build your spotter.**

  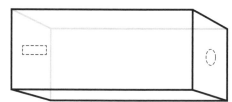

  1. Tape a sheet of paper inside the box at one end.

  2. Cut a 1-inch-by-4-inch view port on the long side of the box about 1 inch from the end with the sheet of paper.

  3. Cut a 1-inch-by-1-inch opening on the short side of the box opposite the end with the sheet of paper.

  4. Securely tape a piece of aluminum foil over the 1-inch opening.

  5. Use a pin to poke a small hole in the aluminum foil.

- **Move the box so that the end with pinhole is pointing at the sun.** Look through the view port to see the sun's image projected on the white paper inside the box!

> To investigate more, consider why the pinhole needs to be so small. What happens if the hole is larger? Why do you need less light coming through the hole in order to see the sun, which is such a great distance away?

# Chapter 4
# Plentiful Planets

NOT ALL PLANETS ARE SOLID LIKE EARTH!

Why are some planets mostly gas while others have rocky terrain?

Planets seem to form differently depending on how far they are from their star, which can make their chemical and physical properties very different from each other.

● ● ● ● ● ● ● ● ●

For thousands of years, ancient people knew planets only as strange, bright stars taking odd paths through the night sky. When the first telescopes brought these planets into view, early astronomers discovered that they were worlds, all circling the sun just like Earth. But what exactly makes something a planet?

For a long time, a planet was any round, large object circling the sun. This fuzzy definition gave us nine planets, listed in their order from the sun: Mercury, Venus, Earth, Mars, Jupiter, Saturn, Uranus, Neptune, and Pluto. This list stayed the same for more than 70 years.

But, with the discovery during the early twenty-first century of several large, distant objects similar to Pluto, astronomers decided on three official membership requirements for the planetary club.

## PLANETARY CLUB MEMBERSHIP REQUIREMENTS

*Established 2006*

To be a planet, an object must do the following:

1. Orbit a star
2. Have pulled itself into a sphere
3. Have cleared its area of other, similar objects

By these rules, eight planets were accepted into the planetary club. Because Pluto has several large neighbors, including Sedna and Eris, it was not allowed in. Instead, the small world became classified as a dwarf planet, along with a few of its neighbors and the giant asteroid called Ceres.

These aren't the only planets in the universe. So far, astronomers have detected more than 4,000 extrasolar planets, or exoplanets, circling other stars. And more are discovered almost every day. In fact, it's likely that most stars have at least one planet, meaning hundreds of billions of exoplanets could exist in the Milky Way alone!

Most of the alien planetary systems discovered so far look very different from our own solar system. Hot, Jupiter-like giant planets orbit their stars much closer than Mercury orbits the sun. Large, rocky super-Earths seem to be common, as are smallish, gassy mini-Neptunes. Just a few planets seem to be about the same size and mass as Earth.

While most alien planets seem to be very different from the planets in our solar system, astronomers think they all formed the same way—from a spinning disk of gas and dust surrounding a young star.

The loss of our ninth planet made many people unhappy. Mike Brown, the planetary scientist whose work led to Pluto's demotion, talks about the controversy in this NPR radio interview.

 why Pluto got demoted

Our solar system might even include another large planet! By studying the orbits of distant dwarf planets, some astronomers think a planet 10 times larger than Earth might lurk in the dark outer edges of the solar system. Although it hasn't been found yet, you can follow the search here!

 find Planet Nine

# HOW PLANETS FORM

Like everything in the universe, planets start out small. About 4.6 billion years ago, our corner of the galaxy was a vast solar nebula left over from the death of an ancient star. Inside the nebula, a large cloud of gas and dust pulled itself together, eventually collapsing to form a new star—the sun. As the young sun grew brighter, it wrapped the rest of the cloud around it into a spinning accretion disk, where the seeds of our solar system took shape.

Inside the turning disk, tiny grains of dust clumped together, gradually becoming countless city-sized boulders called planetesimals.

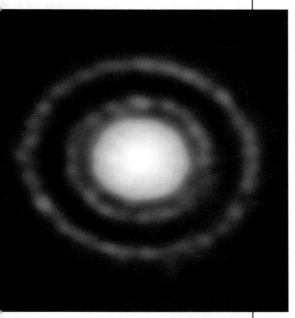

A protoplanetary disc named AS 209

Credit: ALMA (ESO/NAOJ/NRAO)/D. Fedele et al.

In the warmer, inner disk close to the sun, planetesimals formed from elements that don't melt easily, including rock and metals such as nickel and iron. In the cooler outer disk, planetesimals also contained lots of ices, including methane, ammonia, and frozen water.

Millions of planetesimals swarmed around the dusty early solar system, gradually growing larger as they collided and combined with each other. After a few hundred thousand years, most of the planetesimals had combined to form protoplanets, large planetary embryos thousands of miles across.

As they grew, the protoplanets began to differentiate, with gravity pulling their heaviest elements to their centers to form cores. Protoplanets close to the sun formed dense cores of iron and nickel surrounded by molten rock. These were the beginnings of the terrestrial planets, those rocky worlds that include Earth.

In the outer solar system, protoplanets grew cores of rock surrounded by massive amounts of slushy ices made of ammonia, methane, and water. The strong gravity of these larger worlds also collected the gases pushed away from the sun by the solar wind, giving them huge, puffy atmospheres of hydrogen and helium. These outer protoplanets quickly grew into gas giants—large planets made mostly of hydrogen and helium.

But, instead of just eight planets, the early solar system probably had dozens of protoplanets, all trying to make room for themselves. Violent collisions were common, destroying some and tossing others out of the solar system. For about a billion years, the remaining protoplanets battled. These became the planets we know today, neatly divided into the inner and outer planets.

## ROCKING THE INNER PLANETS

Although they are very different worlds, the inner planets have several common features. They are all rocky planets with solid surfaces, dense cores made of iron and nickel, and a rocky layer in between called the mantle. All the inner planets except Mercury have significant atmospheres, but only Earth has the right conditions for liquid water—and life.

Just 36 million miles from the blazing sun, Mercury is a world of extremes. The tiny planet is the smallest in our solar system, a little greater than one-third the diameter of Earth and smaller than a few moons. Without a protective atmosphere, Mercury slowly roasts in the glare of the nearby sun, turning on its axis once every 88 days. The sunlit surface is heated to 700 kelvin (more than 800 degrees Fahrenheit), while the nightside drops to a frigid 93 kelvin (-292 degrees Fahrenheit).

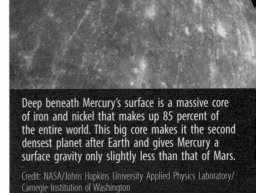

Deep beneath Mercury's surface is a massive core of iron and nickel that makes up 85 percent of the entire world. This big core makes it the second densest planet after Earth and gives Mercury a surface gravity only slightly less than that of Mars.

Credit: NASA/Johns Hopkins University Applied Physics Laboratory/Carnegie Institution of Washington

## MERCURY

| Discovered | Ancient peoples |
|---|---|
| Distance from sun | 0.387 AU |
| Length of year | 88 Earth days |
| Length of day | 58.6 Earth days |
| Mass | 0.055 times Earth's mass |
| Diameter | 3,032 miles |
| Gravity | 0.378 times Earth's gravity |
| Atmosphere | Traces of hydrogen, helium, oxygen |
| Known moons | None |

To learn more about Mercury, read the articles at this website.

 NASA Mercury overview

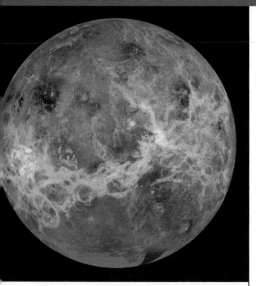

Venus's young, smooth surface has few craters, suggesting it's been reshaped by massive lava flows in the recent past. Venus might even have active volcanoes today.

Credit: NASA/Jet Propulsion Laboratory-Caltech

## VENUS

| Discovered | Ancient peoples |
|---|---|
| Distance from sun | 0.723 AU |
| Length of year | 224.7 Earth days |
| Length of day | 243 Earth days |
| Mass | 0.815 times Earth's mass |
| Diameter | 7,521 miles |
| Gravity | 0.907 times Earth's gravity |
| Atmosphere | Carbon dioxide |
| Known moons | None |

 To learn more about Venus, read the articles at this website.

NASA Venus overview

Although it's a hot, sun-scorched world, Mercury has a few surprises. Spacecraft have found deposits of water ice hidden in the shadows of craters at its north pole, where sunlight can never reach it.

Because it's nearly the same size and mass as Earth, Venus is sometimes called Earth's twin. However, on the surface, the two planets couldn't be more different. Venus is a hellish world with a hot, thick, carbon dioxide atmosphere 92 times denser than Earth's. Hiding beneath the thick clouds and sulfuric acid rain is a singed surface with temperatures reaching 735 kelvin (864 degrees Fahrenheit), making Venus the hottest planet in the solar system.

Exploring space is hard, but exploring the surface of Venus might be harder! The longest-lived probe survived less than two hours on Venus's surface. The few images that we have show a dark and desolate world.

Planetary scientists think that at some point in Venus's past, it was struck by a massive object that tipped it upside-down, giving it a backward, or retrograde, rotation. This collision might also be responsible for the planet's incredibly long day, which is longer than its year. Despite their differences today, Venus may have been more like Earth in the distant past. Scientists think Venus could have had oceans, but as carbon dioxide built up in its atmosphere, all water boiled away due to a runaway greenhouse effect.

Earth sits in the middle of the sun's habitable zone, an area around a star that's the right temperature for liquid water to exist at a planet's surface. Not too hot and not too cold, Earth has deep oceans and rocky continents all wrapped in a protective atmosphere that make it the only planet in the universe known to support life.

Earth is home to millions of species, from tiny bacteria to the giant blue whale. During billions of years, life has evolved and adapted to exist almost everywhere on the planet's surface. While most living things are found in the oceans and on the surface, scientists have found life miles underground and even in the upper reaches of the atmosphere.

Unlike the other terrestrial planets, Earth has a powerful magnetic field that protects its atmosphere and surface from deadly cosmic radiation. Earth is also the only planet with tectonic plates, massive parts of the crust that fit together like puzzle pieces. Moving slowly during millions of years, they constantly reshape the planet's surface.

By studying Earth, scientists have learned a lot about other planets. Understanding our home planet can also help us search for life on other worlds, both inside and outside the solar system.

> Unlike the other terrestrial planets, Earth is also home to one very large satellite you might be familiar with. Because they're somewhat similar in size, some scientists consider the Earth and the moon to be a double planet system.

A unique view of Earth and the moon from the DSCOVR spacecraft. Everything that has ever happened during human history happened right here!

Credit: NASA/NOAA

## EARTH

| Discovered | Ancient peoples |
|---|---|
| Distance from sun | 1 AU |
| Length of year | 365.25 days |
| Length of day | 24 hours |
| Mass | 1.32 x 10^25 pounds |
| Diameter | 7,926 miles |
| Gravity | 1 Earth gravity |
| Atmosphere | Nitrogen, oxygen |
| Known moons | 1 |

To learn more about Earth, read the articles at this website.

🔍 NASA Earth overview

The Mars Science Laboratory, also known as *Curiosity*, takes a selfie from Gale crater as a massive dust storm rages.

Credit: NASA/JPL-Caltech/MSSS

## MARS

| Discovered | Ancient peoples |
|---|---|
| Distance from sun | 1.52 AU |
| Length of year | 687 Earth days |
| Length of day | 24 hours, 37 minutes |
| Mass | 0.107 times Earth's mass |
| Diameter | 4,220 miles |
| Gravity | 0.377 times Earth's gravity |
| Atmosphere | Carbon dioxide |
| Known moons | 2 |

To learn more about Mars, read the articles at this website.

 NASA Mars overview

Mars sits at the outer limits of the sun's habitable zone. It is a cold and dry planet. Its chilliness comes partly from its greater distance from the sun and partly because of its thin atmosphere. At the surface, Mars's carbon dioxide atmosphere is 100 times thinner than Earth's, making it unable to trap heat.

But the "red planet," which gets its nickname from the red iron oxide in its soil, might not have always been so cold and dry. Rovers and satellites have found evidence that water used to flow across the surface, carving out massive rivers, lakes, and even coastlines. However, without the protection of a magnetic field, most of Mars's water and atmosphere was stripped away by the sun, leaving it a dry and frozen world.

Temperatures on Mars can reach as high as 294 kelvin (70 degrees Fahrenheit) near its equator, but the average temperature is a frosty 211 kelvin (-80 degrees Fahrenheit).

Although Mars appears lifeless today, it's possible life existed there in the past—and may still live deep beneath the surface today.

## THE OUTER PLANETS: GAS GIANTS

Beyond the terrestrial planets are the largest planets in the solar system, the gas giants. Gas giants are made mostly of hydrogen and helium. Instead of having a solid surface, these huge worlds have swirling layers of clouds that gradually give way to dense liquid layers surrounding rocky cores. All of the gas giants in the solar system have several moons, and some of those moons are just as interesting as the planets they orbit.

With more than twice the mass of all the other planets put together, Jupiter dominates the solar system. The fifth planet from the sun is best known for its colorful bands of clouds, giant moons, and an Earth-sized, centuries-old storm called the Great Red Spot.

If you could dive beneath the cloud tops on Jupiter, the increasing temperature and pressure would eventually lead to a vast sea of liquid metallic hydrogen squeezing an Earth-sized, rocky core.

The king of the planets is also home to at least 79 moons, including the giant Galilean satellites. Ganymede, with a diameter of 3,274 miles, is the largest satellite in the solar system and wider than the planet Mercury. Io has more than 400 active volcanoes on its surface and is the solar system's most volcanically active object.

In the search for life beyond Earth, Europa is one of the most exciting places to explore. Miles beneath its smooth, icy crust is a vast ocean of water that just might have the right conditions to support life. Astrobiologists hope to explore Europa in detail with the Europa Clipper mission, which should launch in the 2020s.

A close-up of Jupiter from the *JUNO* spacecraft. Check out the mesmerizing, swirling clouds! The Great Red Spot is visible in the upper left.

Credit: NASA/JPL-Caltech/SwRI/MSSS/Kevin M. Gill © (CC BY 3.0)

## JUPITER

| | |
|---|---|
| Discovered | Ancient peoples |
| Distance from sun | 5.2 AU |
| Length of year | 11.9 Earth years |
| Length of day | 9.9 hours |
| Mass | 317.8 times Earth's mass |
| Diameter | 88,846 miles |
| Gravity | 2.36 times Earth's gravity |
| Atmosphere | Hydrogen, helium |
| Known moons | 79 |

To learn more about Jupiter, read the articles at this website.

NASA Jupiter overview

Jupiter's icy satellite Europa

Credit: NASA/JPL-Caltech/ Kevin M. Gill

Saturn's rings are spectacular. Formed about 100 million years ago, they're slowly falling onto the cloud tops below. In a hundred million years, they'll be completely gone!

Credit: NASA/JPL-Caltech/Space Science Institute

## SATURN

| Discovered | Ancient peoples |
|---|---|
| Distance from sun | 9.58 AU |
| Length of year | 29.4 Earth years |
| Length of day | 10.7 hours |
| Mass | 95.2 times Earth's mass |
| Diameter | 74,898 miles |
| Gravity | 0.916 times Earth's gravity |
| Atmosphere | Hydrogen, helium |
| Known moons | 82 |

To learn more about Saturn and its moons, read the articles at this website.

 NASA Saturn overview

Saturn, the second-largest planet in the solar system, is the farthest planet you can see without a telescope. Like Jupiter, Saturn probably has a liquid metallic hydrogen ocean around a large, rocky core.

With a telescope you can easily see Saturn's most amazing feature—its spectacular set of rings. Saturn's rings are mostly chunks of water ice that range in size from snowflakes to car-sized boulders. Despite stretching more than 175,000 miles across, the rings are just 3,200 feet thick. They're thought to be the remains of shattered moons that either collided or were torn apart by Saturn's gravity.

Circling Saturn are 82 moons, more than any other planet. The largest, Titan, is the second biggest moon in the solar system and the only one with a thick atmosphere. In fact, the nitrogen and methane atmosphere is 1.4 times denser than Earth's!

Beneath the orange haze, liquid methane falls on Titan like water falls on Earth, gathering into rivers, lakes, and seas. But, with a surface temperature of -238 degrees Fahrenheit (-150 degrees Celsius), Titan is no place you'd want to swim. While it might resemble the Earth in many ways, it's probably much too cold to support life as we know it. Another of Saturn's moons, Enceladus, might be a better place to look.

Like Europa, Enceladus is a bright, icy moon with a very smooth surface. Scientists have seen water ice erupting from several cracks near Enceladus's south pole, hinting at a vast warm ocean beneath the surface. Scientists think this tiny moon might be a good place to look in the hunt for life beyond Earth.

Far beyond Saturn is Uranus, the coldest planet in the solar system and one we know little about.

Like Jupiter and Saturn, Uranus is made mostly of hydrogen and helium, but it probably gets its unique blue-green coloring from clouds of methane, ammonia, and water ice. Far beneath the frigid clouds, a salty ocean of water and ammonia likely surrounds a slushy core of ice and rock.

Uranus's most unique feature is its extreme 97-degree axial tilt. Astronomers aren't sure how Uranus ended up on its side, but they suspect it was the result of a massive collision long ago. As a result, each pole spends half of Uranus's 84-year orbit in sunlight, the other half in darkness.

Too faint to be see with the naked eye, distant Uranus was the first planet to be discovered by telescope. Its discovery doubled the size of the known universe when it was first spotted in 1781.

Of Uranus's 27 known moons, the most interesting might be tiny Miranda. At 292 miles wide, it's barely large enough to mold itself into a sphere. Its surface is crisscrossed by long grooves and cracks that look stitched together in a random patchwork, earning the little satellite the nickname the "Frankenstein moon." Miranda also has giant, 12-mile-deep canyons, easily the deepest in the solar system.

Neptune is the farthest planet from the sun. It is a cold, distant, and poorly understood planet. Neptune seems to be built a lot like Uranus, consisting mostly of hydrogen and helium with clouds of ammonia, methane, and water ice giving it its vivid blue color. A salty mixture of ammonia and methane ices mixed with water likely wraps around a slushy core of rock and ice.

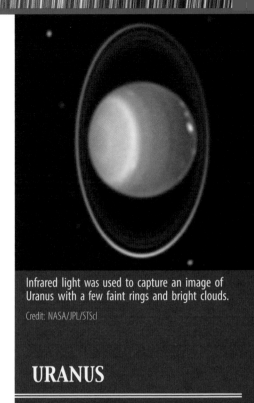

Infrared light was used to capture an image of Uranus with a few faint rings and bright clouds.

Credit: NASA/JPL/STScI

## URANUS

| | |
|---|---|
| Discovered | 1781 |
| Distance from sun | 19.2 AU |
| Length of year | 83.7 Earth years |
| Length of day | 17.2 hours |
| Mass | 14.5 times Earth's mass |
| Diameter | 31,763 miles |
| Gravity | 0.89 times Earth's gravity |
| Atmosphere | Hydrogen, helium |
| Known moons | 27 |

To learn more about Uranus, read the articles at this website.

 NASA Uranus overview

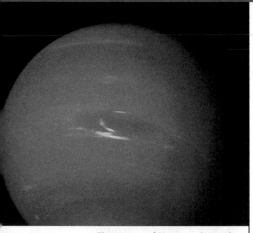

This image of Neptune shows the Great Dark Spot, a giant storm similar to Jupiter's Great Red Spot.

Credit: NASA/JPL

## NEPTUNE

| | |
|---|---|
| Discovered | 1846 |
| Distance from sun | 30.1 AU |
| Length of year | 163.7 Earth years |
| Length of day | 16.1 hours |
| Mass | 17.1 times Earth's mass |
| Diameter | 30,775 miles |
| Gravity | 1.12 times Earth's gravity |
| Atmosphere | Hydrogen, helium |
| Known moons | 14 |

To learn more about Neptune, read the articles at this website.

 NASA Neptune overview

Neptune has 14 moons. Triton is the largest and also one of the oddest. Like Europa and Enceladus, Triton may contain liquid water beneath its bright and icy surface.

More massive than the rest of Neptune's moons combined, Triton orbits Neptune in the opposite direction of all its other satellites. This retrograde orbit means that Triton is likely a captured dwarf planet, a small icy world like Pluto that simply came too close to Neptune in the distant past.

Unfortunately for Triton, this backward motion is slowly drawing it into Neptune. In a few billion years, it will likely be torn apart by Neptune's gravity, probably becoming a massive system of rings.

## ALIEN WORLDS: EXOPLANETS

Have you ever wanted to visit an alien world? Maybe catch a double sunset or ride a wave on an alien ocean? Alien planets are a staple of science fiction, and for a long time, sci-fi was the only place you could find them—but not anymore. Today, we know of thousands of exoplanets circling other stars, each with their own unique story. Some are gas giants like Jupiter, others are small rocky worlds like Earth, and many are somewhere in between.

Finding exoplanets isn't easy. Spying the faint glow of a distant exoplanet next to the brilliant glare of a star is like trying to see a candle held next to a spotlight from miles away. So, instead of searching for them directly, astronomers look for the effect exoplanets have on the stars they orbit.

Stars hold planets in their orbits thanks to their powerful gravitational pull, but a planet's gravity also pulls on its star. The slight tug from a planet can make stars wobble slightly, changing how their light looks to astronomers on Earth. This tiny change in light means there's a good chance a hidden planet is tugging on its star. This way of searching for exoplanets is called the radial velocity method.

Another way to hunt for alien worlds is to use the transit method. If an exoplanet transits, or passes directly between Earth and a star, a tiny amount of the star's light is blocked, like a distant, alien eclipse. If astronomers see a regular dip in the light from a star, it could mean an exoplanet is there.

The transit method has found thousands of exoplanets, most of them discovered in just the last few years by the Kepler Space Telescope. Astronomers think a new, space-based observatory called TESS (Transiting Exoplanet Survey Satellite) will find even more.

Together, both methods have found a fraction of the hundreds of billions of planets that could be in the Milky Way alone! So far, few planets have looked like Earth. Most have been large gas giants similar to Jupiter and Saturn. Others have been mini-Neptunes, smaller than our eighth planet but with thick, puffy atmospheres.

Finding another Earth isn't just about size. A truly habitable world not only needs to be the right size, it also needs to be the right distance from its star.

> Of the few Earth-sized worlds found so far, only a few sit within their star's habitable zone. And, of those, one in particular stands out.

Astronomers have detected thousands of exoplanets, and more are being found all the time. Want to keep up with the latest discoveries of exoplanets? Check out NASA's Exoplanet Exploration website here.

 NASA exoplanets

## COSMIC CONCEPT

The first planet circling a star like the sun was found in 1995. The planet 51 Pegasi-b is a hot Jupiter, a large gas giant orbiting its star closer than Mercury orbits the sun.

An artist's impression of the TRAPPIST-1 planets. TRAPPIST-1e is fourth from the left.

Credit: NASA/JPL-Caltech

## TRAPPIST-1E

| Planet type | Terrestrial |
|---|---|
| Diameter | Approximately 91% of Earth |
| Mass | Approximately 77% of Earth |
| Surface gravity | Approximately 93% of Earth |
| Distance from star | Approximately .029 AU (2,695,718 miles) |
| Surface temperature | Approximately 246 kelvin (-16.9 degrees Fahrenheit) if there's no atmosphere |
| Atmosphere | Unknown, but not thick like a gas giant |
| Year | 6.1 Earth days |
| Day | Same as a year due to tidal locking |

Learn more about the TRAPPIST-1 system at this website.

NASA 10 things TRAPPIST-1

# TRAPPIST-1E

A little more than 39 light-years away is a small, dim star visible only with the help of a powerful telescope. TRAPPIST-1 is a red dwarf, just a tenth of the sun's mass and not much bigger than Jupiter. On its own, it isn't a very interesting star. What makes it remarkable are the seven Earth-sized planets that circle it.

In the TRAPPIST-1 system, everything is small. The star system has no gas giants—all seven of the planets in this system are small rocky worlds like those in our inner solar system. And all of them orbit their star closer than Mercury orbits the sun. But because TRAPPIST-1 puts out only a tiny fraction of the sun's energy, they're not hellish, roasted worlds. In fact, three of the worlds sit comfortably in TRAPPIST-1's habitable zone.

One of them, TRAPPIST-1e, is the most Earth-like planet discovered so far.

TRAPPIST-1e is a terrestrial world like Earth, with nearly the same diameter, density, and surface gravity as our home planet. And even though it's 34 times closer to its star than Earth is to the sun, it even has about the same surface temperature as Earth. In fact, if you could stand on TRAPPIST-1e, it might feel a lot like being on Earth! But the view would be very different.

TRAPPIST-1e is probably tidally locked to its star, meaning that one side is in constant sunlight while the other is left in darkness. On the day side, the deep red star would hang motionless in the sky, appearing much larger than the sun does from Earth. This wouldn't be the only strange sight.

Because the planets in the TRAPPIST-1 system are so close to each other, you would have incredible views of them as they moved in their orbits.

With the planet split evenly between day and night, temperatures could be extreme on both sides, with one hemisphere roasting under relentless heat and the other covered in ice. But, on the border between day and night, the environment might be more Earth-like, creating a narrow, habitable ring circling the planet from pole to pole. A thick atmosphere could also help even out differences in temperature around the planet.

However, just because the conditions for life might exist on TRAPPIST-1e, it doesn't mean life is likely. Small stars such as the red dwarf TRAPPIST-1 are often seen belching powerful and dangerous solar flares from their surfaces, which could roast nearby planets or even strip away their atmospheres.

Of the hundreds of billions of possible planets in the Milky Way, it might not be too long before we find a planet even more like Earth. And then, maybe, we'll find life!

## VOCAB LAB

Write down what you think each word means. What root words can you find to help you? What does the context of the word tell you?

**astrobiologist, gas giant, habitable zone, molten, planetesimal, protoplanet,** and **terrestrial planet**.

Compare your definitions with those of your friends or classmates. Did you all come up with the same meanings? Turn to the text and glossary if you need help.

### KEY QUESTIONS

- **Why are scientists eager to find planets similar to Earth that could support life?**
- **What are some of the challenges of exploring other planets?**

## TEXT TO WORLD

Do you enjoy science fiction? What are some questions that sci-fi raises for you?

# MODEL AN ALIEN SOLAR SYSTEM

The TRAPPIST-1 system is closer in size to Jupiter and its moons than it is to the sun and its eight planets. Can you build a model of the TRAPPIST-1 system?

Want to help discover planets around other stars? The TESS (Transiting Exoplanet Survey Satellite) telescope is scanning stars for tiny dips in brightness that might signal an exoplanet. And scientists need your help! Check out this website to join the hunt!

zooniverse planet hunters

- **Take a look at a comparison between Jupiter and the TRAPPIST-1 system at this website.**

Spitzer TRAPPIST-1 compared

- **To create a scale model, research the sizes and distances between the objects in the TRAPPIST-1 system.** This website has information about the size and orbits of the seven TRAPPIST-1 planets.

TRAPPIST-1 planet data

- **As you design your model, ask yourself these questions.**

  - How big should you make your model?

  - What materials will you use?

  - How will you display your model?

- **Build the model out of materials you choose.** How does it come out? Can you use it to explain the TRAPPIST-1 system? How can you improve it so that other people can use it for research?

> To investigate more, consider creating a model that shows both the TRAPPIST-1 and Jupiter systems to scale. What about other exoplanet systems? How might they compare to TRAPPIST-1, Jupiter, or our own solar system?

# Chapter 5 ▷
# The Living Earth

WHAT IS IT THAT MAKES THE EARTH SO SPECIAL?

What makes Earth different than any other known planet?

Earth hits the sweet spot in terms of atmosphere. Other planets might support life, but it would probably be very different.

● ● ● ● ● ● ● ● ●

**Earth is a pretty fantastic place. Covered in wide continents and deep oceans and wrapped in a protective atmosphere, it's the only home we've ever known. Besides a few short trips to the moon, all human history has happened right here, on a tiny blue planet circling an average star in a quiet corner of an unremarkable galaxy. What makes Earth unique is that nearly every inch of it is covered with life.**

From the tiniest bacteria to the biggest blue whales, our planet is home to millions of different species of living organisms and is the only place we know of in the universe that's currently supporting life. But what makes our tiny blue planet, circling an unremarkable star in an unremarkable part of an unremarkable galaxy, such a great place to live?

To understand what makes Earth so special, it helps to think of our world as a giant, planet-sized puzzle with four pieces, or spheres—the geosphere, atmosphere, hydrosphere, and biosphere.

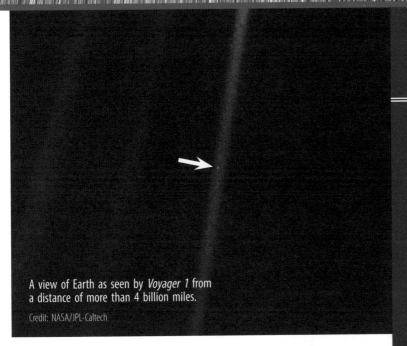

A view of Earth as seen by *Voyager 1* from a distance of more than 4 billion miles.

Credit: NASA/JPL-Caltech

## HOME

"That's here. That's home. That's us. On it everyone you love, everyone you know, everyone you ever heard of, every human being who ever was, lived out their lives. The aggregate of our joy and suffering, thousands of confident religions, ideologies, and economic doctrines, every hunter and forager, every hero and coward, every creator and destroyer of civilization, every king and peasant, every young couple in love, every mother and father, hopeful child, inventor and explorer, every teacher of morals, every corrupt politician, every 'superstar,' every 'supreme leader,' every saint and sinner in the history of our species lived there—on a mote of dust suspended in a sunbeam."

—Carl Sagan, *Pale Blue Dot*, 1994

## THE GEOSPHERE

The geosphere is the foundation that all the other spheres are built upon. It stretches from deep within the center of Earth all the way to the top of the tallest mountain and contains all the rocks, minerals, and metals in between.

In the center of Earth is a 2,883-mile-wide ball of metal called the core. The hottest and densest part of the planet, the core is made of two parts, an inner core and an outer core.

Squeezed by the weight of Earth around it, the blistering inner core is a solid, super-dense ball of nickel and iron. Under less pressure, the cooler outer core is a spinning mix of liquid nickel and iron surrounding the inner core. The outer core's rotation generates Earth's protective magnetic field. Like an invisible shield, it screens us from the sun's steady stream of solar wind. Without this protective bubble, Earth's atmosphere would slowly blow away, exposing the surface to deadly radiation.

### COSMIC CONCEPT

The sun emits many tons of electrically charged particles every second. This flow of particles from the sun's surface streaming out into space in all directions is called the solar wind.

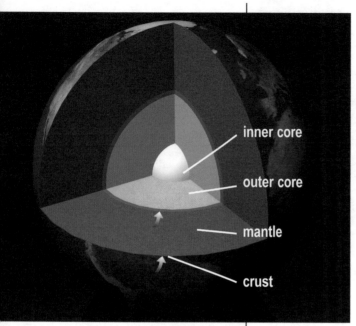

The layers of the earth

Credit: Dave Jarvis, James Hastings-Trew (CC BY 2.5)

Above the core is a thick, dense layer of rock called the mantle. More than 1,800 miles deep, the mantle stretches between the hot core and Earth's surface and makes up more than three-quarters of the entire planet. While it's mostly solid, the tremendous heat causes the mantle to slowly flow like a liquid. As millions of years pass by, convection in the mantle carries warm rock toward the surface while cooler rock sinks. The constant motion of the mantle is part of what drives changes on Earth's surface.

The crust is the outer layer of the geosphere and what we think of as Earth's surface. Compared to the rest of the planet, the crust is incredibly thin, just 25 miles deep beneath continents and only three miles thick under the oceans. Although it might look like a solid shell, the crust is made of more than a dozen large, slowly moving pieces called tectonic plates.

Powered by the warm, rolling mantle below, these giant puzzle pieces are always colliding, sliding, and spreading apart in slow motion, causing earthquakes and volcanoes. During millions and billions of years, their movement has rearranged Earth's surface, shaping the oceans and continents that exist today.

## THE ATMOSPHERE

Starting at Earth's crust and stretching for hundreds of miles into space is the atmosphere. It surrounds the planet and is a mix of gases—78 percent nitrogen, 21 percent oxygen, and small amounts of carbon dioxide and other elements.

## COSMIC CONCEPT

At about 5,700 kelvin (9,806 degrees Fahrenheit) the inner core of Earth is hotter than the surface of the sun. Although it's more than hot enough to melt the iron and nickel it's made of, the tremendous pressure surrounding the inner core keeps it solid.

The atmosphere is essential for life on Earth. Besides keeping the surface warm by trapping the sun's energy, the atmosphere also acts like sunscreen, blocking much of the sun's harmful ultraviolet rays.

Closest to the surface is the dense troposphere, which makes up about 75 percent of Earth's atmosphere. This is where nearly all our weather occurs, including tornadoes, hurricanes, winter storms, and afternoon showers.

About six miles above Earth's surface, the troposphere gives way to the stratosphere. Passenger jets fly into this less-dense layer.

The stratosphere is home to the protective ozone layer that shields Earth's surface from the sun's ultraviolet radiation.

The layer above the stratosphere, stretching from a height of 31 miles to about 53 miles, is the chilly mesosphere. Too thin for airplanes to fly in but too dense for satellites, the mesosphere is difficult to study, but with temperatures around -155 kelvin (-180 degrees Fahrenheit), scientists believe the mesosphere is the coldest place on Earth.

Above 53 miles is the thermosphere, which many people consider to be the edge of space. The thermosphere is a strangely hot layer, where temperatures can reach as high as 1,755 kelvin (2,700 degrees Fahrenheit). Because of this high heat, the air molecules are far apart, which means anything passing through the troposphere doesn't feel the heat. And that's a good thing— the thermosphere is where astronauts aboard the International Space Station (ISS) orbit Earth.

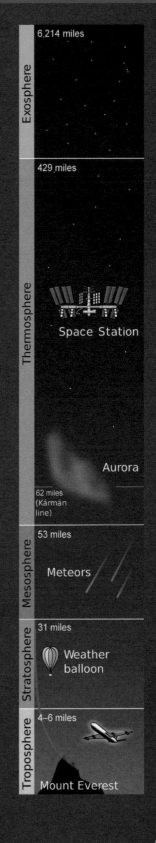

Exosphere

6,214 miles

429 miles

Thermosphere

Space Station

Aurora

62 miles
(Kármán
line)

Mesosphere

53 miles

Meteors

Stratosphere

31 miles

Weather balloon

Troposphere

4–6 miles

Mount Everest

The exosphere is the final layer of Earth's atmosphere, starting around 300 miles above the planet's surface and gradually fading away to space.

Besides providing warmth and breathable air for living organisms, the atmosphere is also the reason we have liquid water on Earth's surface.

Without the gentle pressure of the atmosphere, water couldn't exist as liquid and Earth wouldn't have a hydrosphere.

# THE HYDROSPHERE

Water is an essential part of life on Earth. All living things need water to survive—this substance helps organisms carry nutrients, break down food, get rid of waste, and keep cool. Even our own bodies are more than 75 percent water! Unlike any other planet we know of, Earth has water that can exist as a solid, liquid, or a gas as part of the hydrosphere.

The hydrosphere contains all the water on Earth in all its forms. Whether it's on the surface, in the atmosphere, or deep underground, all of it is constantly moving and recycling through the hydrologic cycle.

As energy from the sun warms liquid water on Earth's surface, the water evaporates and becomes water vapor. That vapor is carried up to the atmosphere, where it cools, condensing into droplets to form clouds. When these drops of water become large enough, they fall as precipitation and start the cycle again. Without the hydrosphere and the hydrologic cycle, it's hard to imagine how life on Earth could even exist!

## COSMIC CONCEPT

It's hard to say exactly where Earth's atmosphere ends and space begins, but the most commonly accepted "edge" of space is the Kármán line (you can see this line on the graphic on the previous page). Named after Theodore von Kármán (1881–1963), a Hungarian-American physicist, the Kármán line is an altitude of 62 miles (100 kilometers). Some scientists argue that the exosphere stretches all the way to the moon!

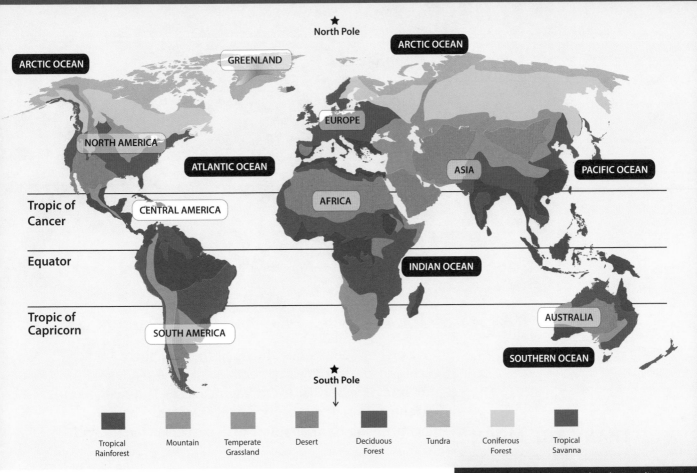

North Pole

ARCTIC OCEAN

GREENLAND

ARCTIC OCEAN

EUROPE

NORTH AMERICA

ATLANTIC OCEAN

ASIA

PACIFIC OCEAN

AFRICA

**Tropic of Cancer**

CENTRAL AMERICA

**Equator**

INDIAN OCEAN

**Tropic of Capricorn**

SOUTH AMERICA

AUSTRALIA

SOUTHERN OCEAN

South Pole

| | | | | | | | |
|---|---|---|---|---|---|---|---|
| Tropical Rainforest | Mountain | Temperate Grassland | Desert | Deciduous Forest | Tundra | Coniferous Forest | Tropical Savanna |

A biome is a natural area with a distinct climate and with plants and animals adapted for life there. Explore the world map to discover where Earth's major biomes are located. Notice how one biome rolls into another.

# THE BIOSPHERE

Every living thing on our planet, including plants, animals, and even the tiniest microorganisms, are part of the biosphere. The biosphere is the complex web of all living things, and it connects all the spheres of Earth.

The biosphere stretches from high in the atmosphere down to the deepest ocean trenches, from the tallest mountain to deep beneath the crust, and everywhere in between. Because life is found pretty much everywhere we look, the biosphere is part of and depends on all the other spheres to function.

## THANK THE MOON

Why do we have seasons? It's not due to Earth's distance from the sun, but to the 23.5-degree tilt of the planet's axis. When the Northern Hemisphere is tilted toward the sun, it is summer in that hemisphere and people south of the equator have winter. The opposite is true when the Southern Hemisphere is tilted toward the sun. Scientists suspect that the collision that formed the moon also tipped Earth, giving us seasons.

Millions of species currently call the biosphere home, living in diverse environments across the planet. To study life and all the different places it thrives, scientists sort the biosphere into biomes, where living things have adapted to a particular terrain and climate.

Biomes can be dry deserts, lush forests, wide grasslands, chilly tundra, oceans, lakes, or flowing rivers. Within biomes, groups of living and non-living things create ecosystems that maintain a balance of water, food, nutrients, and energy. Biomes can contain lots of different ecosystems, all working to benefit each other. But how did they all get here?

## THE FORMATION OF EARTH

Like everything else in the solar system, Earth got its start about 4.5 billion years ago when the sun formed a huge collapsing cloud of dust and gas. As a few million years went by, the tiny mote of dust that would become our planet grew bigger, collecting rocks, boulders, and even other planetesimals to become a large proto-Earth.

If we could travel back to this proto-Earth, we wouldn't recognize our own planet. It had no seas, continents, or even breathable air. And for millions of years, the proto-Earth was pummeled by rocks, asteroids, comets, and even other protoplanets.

In fact, Earth was struck its greatest blow when it was sideswiped by a Mars-sized neighbor that astronomers have named Theia. The theory goes that the violent collision vaporized Theia and nearly destroyed Earth, sending pieces of both worlds tumbling into orbit around our fractured planet.

> Eventually, the debris condensed as a new world, forming our small rocky neighbor we call the moon.

Not long after the moon formed, Earth's surface was covered in a sea of hot magma. Huge amounts of carbon dioxide, nitrogen, steam, and molten rock erupted from volcanoes, surrounding the planet with a scalding, toxic atmosphere. After a few hundred million years, the atmosphere cooled enough for water to condense. Rain fell to Earth for the first time. For centuries, the water pooled and collected, forming Earth's first rivers, lakes, and seas. With the arrival of the first oceans around 3.8 billion years ago, Earth was ready for life.

## THE ORIGINS OF LIFE

Life on Earth is amazingly rich and diverse. It's found almost anywhere we look, from deep beneath the ocean to high up in the atmosphere, spread across continents and even far underground. But nobody knows exactly how or when life began. It's one of the biggest questions in science, and people have been trying to find an answer for centuries.

## THE SOUP OF LIFE

In 1952 scientists Stanley Miller (1930–2007) and Harold Urey (1893–1981) showed how organic molecules—carbon-based molecules necessary for life—could be created from the environment of early Earth. A soupy mixture of gases similar to Earth's ancient atmosphere was zapped with electricity, producing amino acids. Amino acids are the building blocks of proteins, the complex organic molecules that all living organisms need to function. To learn more about this amazing experiment, watch this video.

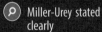 Miller-Urey stated clearly

Stromatolites at Hamelin Pool in Shark Bay, Australia

Credit: Bryn Pinzgauer (CC BY 2.0)

## HELLO, ALIEN!

It's possible that life didn't begin on Earth but hitched a ride here from somewhere else. Panspermia is the theory that life on Earth got its start somewhere else and was brought here by a crashing comet or asteroid. That would make us all aliens! Although the raw materials for life also exist on other planets, such as Mars, the only place we've found any sign of life's beginnings is right here on Earth. So, it's unlikely—but possible—that we're all aliens.

Even though it was a much different place than it is today, ancient Earth had an atmosphere, water, sunlight, and a rocky crust filled with elements—all the raw materials needed for life. Abiogenesis is the theory that the first living organisms arose naturally from these non-living things.

Most scientists believe that just having the right stuff together in the right place at the right time was enough for life to form, but the details of exactly how this happened are still a mystery.

The earliest solid evidence of life comes from stromatolites, fossilized mud and ooze left behind by microorganisms that lived and died in the first oceans about 3.7 billion years ago. The creatures that formed these fossils were single-celled organisms called prokaryotes. Prokaryotes are the most successful organisms to ever live. They're still around today as bacteria and archaea, living in some of the most dangerous environments on Earth.

For more than a billion years, these simple life forms dominated life on Earth. To survive that long on a changing planet, the prokaryotes, like all living things before and since, had to find a way to adapt and change themselves or risk disappearing from Earth forever.

# EVOLUTION

Evolution is the theory that all species change with time. Every plant, animal, and microorganism that exists today is descended from earlier organisms that adapted to new and changing environments. Evolution explains how life started out as very simple, single-celled organisms to become a planet filled with diverse plants and animals.

Evolution works through natural selection, which is sometimes called "survival of the fittest." For a species to survive, it must be able to adapt to changes in its environment, such as the arrival of a dangerous predator or the loss of a source of food. If it can't, it may become extinct.

Natural selection happens when one member of a species is born with slightly different traits, or features, from other members. For example, a bird could be born with a new color that helps hide it from deadly predators, such as cats. These changes come from mutations, small differences in an organism's DNA, that happen by chance.

If a mutation is harmful, those with it are less likely to survive through future generations. But a helpful mutation, one that gives an individual an advantage over other members of its species, is more likely to survive into the future. As time goes by, these small but valuable changes in individuals can create entirely new species that are very different from their ancestors.

The theory of evolution, first described by Charles Darwin (1809–1882), is one of the most important scientific ideas of all time. From biology to chemistry to paleontology, an overwhelming amount of scientific evidence supports evolution. To learn more about this amazing idea and the evidence that supports it, check out this video.

evolution crash course biology

Snowshoe hares evolved the ability to change the color of their fur to white during winter and brown during the summer. Why does this adaptation help them survive? Hint: They live in a snowy climate!

Credit: Dave Doe (CC BY 2.0)

## COSMIC CONCEPT

If you weighed all life on Earth, most of it would be prokaryotes. These small, simple creatures have been on Earth for billions of years!

If you think of genes as a computer program, then DNA is the code. DNA is the genetic code of all living things. It's a very long, thin molecule shaped like a twisted ladder called a double helix. To learn more about DNA and how it works, check out this website.

🔍 Crash Course DNA

One of the biggest evolutionary changes happened about 3 billion years ago, when a species of prokaryotes called cyanobacteria evolved the amazing ability to turn sunlight and carbon dioxide into energy through a process called photosynthesis. These tiny bacteria were so successful they changed the planet by releasing oxygen into the atmosphere. This helpful trait was eventually passed down to plants. Even today, almost all the oxygen in Earth's atmosphere comes from photosynthesis.

# MULTICELLULAR ORGANISMS

Have you ever been part of a team? All complex life on Earth today is made of millions of different cells working together as a single organism. But, 2 billion years ago, teamwork was a new idea.

It might have started when a large prokaryote mistook a smaller one for dinner. Instead of becoming a meal, the swallowed cell got to work feasting on the large cell's waste and turning it into energy. As time passed, these symbiotic cells became part of each other, sharing DNA and eventually evolving into a new kind of organism called a eukaryote.

Eukaryotic cells are more complex than their prokaryotic cousins, with specialized parts for feeding, reproducing, and making energy. During the next billion years, eukaryotic cells began living and working together in larger and larger groups and evolved into the first multicellular organisms.

The new creatures were made of many specialized cells with their own specific tasks, such as performing photosynthesis or ingesting other microorganisms. These patchwork life forms evolved into the first plants and animals on Earth.

Between 1 billion and 600 million years ago, the first plants and animals appeared in the oceans. However, these weren't beautiful flowers or giant sharks with sharp, pointy teeth. The first plants were probably simple green algae, microscopic organisms that are still around today. The first animals were likely small and slow, if they moved at all. They were probably ancient sea sponges, creatures that filter food from water and are also still around today.

But, about 500 million years ago, a massive burst of diversity called the Cambrian Explosion took place. In less than 100 million years, the ancestors of almost all animal species appeared and the first four-limbed vertebrates made their way onto land. These first explorers evolved into all the four-limbed animals we know now, including humans. However, the evolutionary process wasn't easy.

## PROS AND EUKS

Eukaryotes are different from prokaryotes in a few ways. Both kinds of cell have cell walls, DNA, and ribosomes for making proteins. But, unlike prokaryotes, eukaryotes have organelles, specialized parts such as mitochondria, which produce energy for cells, and a nucleus, which keeps DNA safe and organized. To learn more about prokaryotes and eukaryotes, take a look at this video.

 amoeba sisters prokaryotic vs. eukaryotic

Fossil skeleton of a *Diadectes phaseolinus*, an early tetrapod

# EXTINCTION

Extinction is a natural part of evolution. In fact, more than 99 percent of all species that have ever lived have gone extinct. Some evolved into new creatures, while others died out when they were unable to adapt to new environments or living conditions.

Sometimes, entire groups die off in a short period of time, disappearing from Earth forever. These events are called mass extinctions.

Mass extinctions occur when major changes in Earth's environment happen faster than most species can adapt.

At least five mass extinctions have taken place, the largest happening about 250 million years ago, when 95 percent of all living species died out in just 60,000 years. Called the Great Dying, it was the single largest extinction in Earth's history. The Great Dying was likely caused by massive volcanic eruptions, which led to increased temperatures around the planet in a very short time.

Mass extinctions can be devastating, but they can also create opportunities for other species to thrive For more than 200 million years, dinosaurs were the rulers of Earth, dominating the land, air, and sea. Then, about 66 million years ago, the planet was struck by a massive asteroid or comet on what is today the Yucatán Peninsula of Mexico.

Millions of tons of vaporized rock and soil were sent into the atmosphere, blocking out sunlight and plunging the planet into a global winter. At least 75 percent of all life on Earth was wiped out, including all dinosaurs except the ancestors of birds.

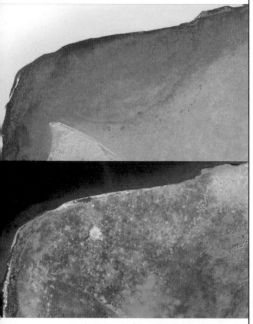

A shaded relief image of the northwest corner of Mexico's Yucatán Peninsula, showing where the asteroid or comet hit

Credit: NASA/JPL

This mass extinction also cleared the way for mammals to reign in their place. Just 10 million years later, our planet had thousands of species of mammals, including the first whales, bats, and our earliest human ancestors.

## HOMO SAPIENS

Without question, human beings are the dominant form of life on Earth today. All of us are members of the species *Homo Sapiens*, which means "wise man" in Latin. Since the first modern humans appeared around 300,000 years ago, we've constructed cities and connected them by road and rail, circled the planet in airplanes, walked on the moon, and uploaded millions of cat videos to the internet. But we owe much knowledge and progress to the achievements of earlier members in our family tree.

> Just 7 million years ago, in Africa, our ancient ancestors split from the ancestors of chimpanzees, our closest living relatives today.

While the ancestors of chimps remained tree climbers, our forebearers left the trees behind to walk on two legs. This led to bipedal ancestors, such as the Australopithecines. While *Australopithecus* was shorter and had a much smaller brain than their human descendants, *Australopithecus* may have been the first primate to make and use tools. This tool-building trait continued with *Homo habilis* ("handy man"), the earliest known member of our human species. *Homo habilis* lived between 2.5 and 1 million years ago and stood taller and had a larger brain than *Australopithecus*. *Homo habilis* left behind many tools carved from bones and rocks.

## COSMIC CONCEPT

If the entire history of Earth were squashed into one year, *Homo sapiens* wouldn't appear until the last hour of the last day of the year—at about 11:30 p.m. on New Year's Eve!

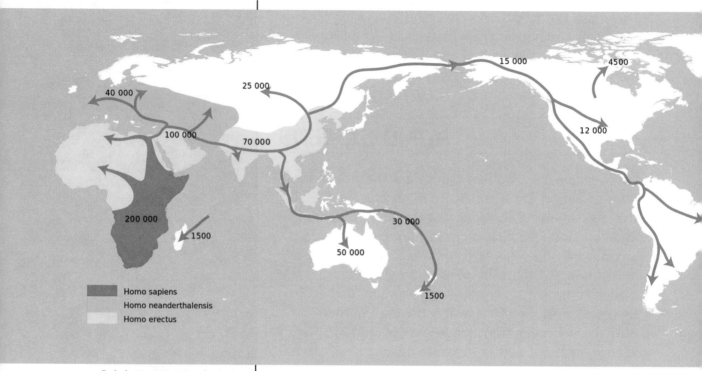

Early human migration, beginning 200,000 years ago in Africa

Homo sapiens
Homo neanderthalensis
Homo erectus

In 2013, Paul Salopek (1962– ) set out on a years-long journey following the path of human migration. You can follow him by reading his articles at this website. Why did he decide to do this? What is the value of this trek?

 Nat Geo Paul Salopek

Another big step on the path to *Homo sapiens* was *Homo erectus* ("upright man"), who lived between 2 million and 500,000 years ago. Although not as tall as modern humans, the bodies and brains of *Homo erectus* were much larger than *Homo habilis*, and their achievements were more advanced. These bright cousins of ours tinkered with more detailed stone tools and weapons and may have been the first of our ancestors to use fire.

The use of fire was an incredible technological advancement.

It allowed our ancestors to keep warm in cool climates, ward off dangerous predators, and cook and preserve meals—all things they'd need to do when they left Africa.

*Homo erectus* was likely the first member of our species to leave Africa, spreading into Europe and as far east as China and Indonesia. But they weren't the last.

The first modern humans emerged in Africa about 300,000 years ago, and if you dressed them in some modern clothes, they'd probably fit right in today. *Homo sapiens* were taller and thinner compared to earlier human ancestors, and their large brains continued to invent, creating spoken languages.

As time passed, they learned to farm, which led to the first villages and large communities.

Around 100 thousand years ago, *Homo sapiens* began moving into Europe and Asia—but other groups of humans were already there. If either Neanderthals (*Homo neanderthalensis*) or Denisovans were alive today, they'd be our closest human relatives. All three human species likely split between 300,000 and 400,000 years ago, with Neanderthals and Denisovans ending up in Europe and Asia and modern humans making the trip a few thousand years later.

Despite the myth that Neanderthals were large, unintelligent cavemen, both Neanderthals and Denisovans weren't that much different from modern humans. They were shorter and stronger, with large noses and thick brow ridges above their eyes. And they were smart, crafting complex tools, using fire, and even creating jewelry and cave paintings.

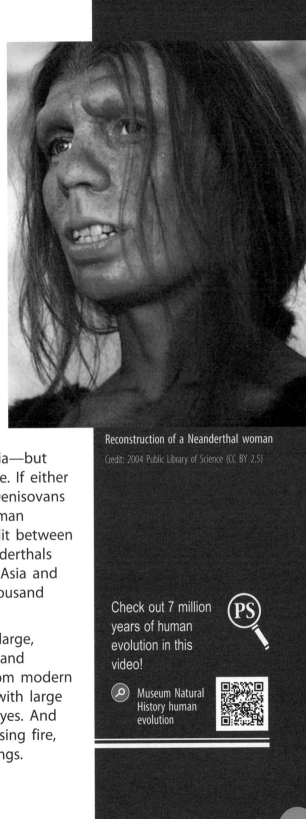

Reconstruction of a Neanderthal woman

Credit: 2004 Public Library of Science (CC BY 2.5)

Check out 7 million years of human evolution in this video!

Museum Natural History human evolution

## VOCAB LAB

Write down what you think each word means. What root words can you find to help you? What does the context of the word tell you?

**biome**, **biosphere**, **cyanobacteria**, **geosphere**, **hydrologic cycle**, **mass extinction**, **symbiotic**, and **thermosphere**.

Compare your definitions with those of your friends or classmates. Did you all come up with the same meanings? Turn to the text and glossary if you need help.

## TEXT TO WORLD

What kind of biome do you live in? What kinds of plants and animals share your ecosystem?

All three species lived together for thousands of years, until around 30,000 to 40,000 years ago, when Neanderthals and Denisovans disappeared. The reason for their extinction is a mystery. It's possible that competition from *Homo sapiens* or a changing climate made it hard for them to survive.

But they're not entirely gone. During the brief time Neanderthals and Denisovans lived near modern humans, they interbred, and some of their ancient DNA lives on. In fact, most people with European ancestry have between 1 and 4 percent Neanderthal DNA, while some people with East Asian ancestry get 3 to 6 percent of their DNA from Denisovans.

And human evolution isn't over. Our species continues to change and evolve on Earth, influenced by our culture and environment. It's possible that millions of years from now, we may have evolved into a new human species altogether!

Earth is a pretty special place, unique in the universe with its ability to support life. But, in the last century, human beings have gained the ability to change the world for better and for worse. How long it stays a good place to live is up to us, as you will read in the next chapter.

### KEY QUESTIONS

- **Can you think of more examples of natural selection? What can we learn from natural adaptation?**

- **What role does extinction play in evolution?**

# MODEL THE SPHERES OF EARTH WITH A TERRARIUM

The four spheres of Earth—the geosphere, hydrosphere, atmosphere, and biosphere—are all connected. Each has a role to play in keeping Earth a friendly environment for life. While Earth is pretty big, you can build your own smaller version of the four spheres with a terrarium.

A terrarium is a collection of live plants, soil, air, and water sealed off from the outside world. It's usually built in a sealable glass or plastic container and needs very little help staying alive as long as it has access to sunlight.

* **In a sealable container, place layers of rocks, activated charcoal (found wherever aquarium supplies are sold), and potting soil.**

* **Time to plant!** Get some miniature plants that won't grow too big for the container. Plants of different shapes, colors, and textures will make your terrarium interesting to look at. Talk with a garden specialist or do research at the library to find out the best kinds of plants. If you need help getting started, check out this link.

climate kids terrarium

* **Think about the following.**

  * What parts of the terrarium represent each of the four spheres of Earth?

  * Unlike regular plants, a terrarium needs very little attention or extra water added. Why do you think this is?

To investigate more, consider what happens to the living planets of the biosphere if you change or alter one of the other spheres. How are they all related and connected?

# Chapter 6 ▶
# Into the Future

WHAT'S IN STORE FOR THE FUTURE OF EARTH?

What are some of the ways the earth, the solar system, or even the universe might end?

ASTEROIDS HAVE HIT US IN THE PAST, AND THAT COULD VERY WELL HAPPEN AGAIN!

IT'S INCREDIBLY FAR IN THE FUTURE, BUT THE SUN WILL GO OUT, JUST LIKE ANY STAR.

AND EARTH'S CLIMATE COULD HAVE A MORE IMMEDIATE IMPACT. THE FUTURE IS SO COMPLICATED!

AND SCIENTIFICALLY AWESOME!!

Everything must come to an end, including the universe! But all of the end-of-days scenarios won't happen until far, far in the future—except for climate change. That is one major change that is barreling down on us with unprecedented speed. It's also the change we have most control over.

● ● ● ● ● ● ● ● ●

**So far, we've found out how the universe got underway with a Big Bang, studied black holes at the hearts of galaxies, discovered how stars shine, and learned what makes Earth such an incredible and—so far—unique place in the universe. But that only takes us up to today.**

What will our universe be like thousands, billions, even trillions of years in the future?

What will happen to the solar system when the sun runs out of fuel? What will happen to the Milky Way when it collides with the Andromeda Galaxy? And will the universe just keep on expanding and cooling forever or is something else in store? Whatever the future holds, it's probably best to start at home.

# KILLER NEOS

You'd never know it, but right now, small, dark objects in the solar system may have Earth in their crosshairs. Since it was formed, Earth has been regularly hit by asteroids and comets. Today, most are a safe distance from us, either in the main asteroid belt or on the outskirts of the solar system in the distant Oort Cloud. However, some of these space rocks make it as close to us as Earth's orbit. Astronomers call them near-Earth objects (NEOs).

Out of the millions of asteroids and trillions of comets in the solar system, NEOs make up only a tiny fraction. So far, astronomers have found and tracked about 18,000 NEOs. Most of them are less than 82 feet wide and would probably vaporize in Earth's atmosphere before they hit the ground. Objects wider than 0.62 mile are much more dangerous, but they are also much rarer. A meteoroid the size of a soccer field hits Earth once every 2,000 years or so.

> The really big rocks in space, the kind that helped wipe out the dinosaurs, only come around every few million years. Fortunately, the bigger an object, the easier it is to detect.

During the last 20 years, astronomers think they've found about 95 percent of all the NEOs larger than 0.62 mile across. In fact, not one of the NEOs spotted so far has even a 1-percent chance of striking Earth within the next century. So, you can mostly relax! While not all the dangerous objects in the solar system are known, more are being discovered and monitored every day. But, if we do find an NEO, can we do anything about it?

Want to know more about finding, tracking, and studying asteroids? Check out NASA's planetary defense website.

 NASA planetary defense

You can also listen to Season 2 of NASA's *On a Mission* podcasts here.

 NASA On Mission podcast

# STOPPING AN ASTEROID

Unlike in the movies, blowing up an asteroid or comet would probably be a bad idea. Some space rocks are just a loose pile of rubble. Blowing them up could turn them into thousands of smaller asteroids still on the same path toward Earth.

If a dangerous object is headed for Earth, the most important thing is time. While moving an object the size of a mountain isn't easy, the earlier we find it, the less energy it will take to deflect it and change its course.

One option would be to ram an approaching object at high speed—like cosmic bumper cars—in the hope of changing its course. But this method, called kinetic impaction, could also result in many smaller chunks of rock heading in our direction. Another way to move an asteroid is to detonate a nuclear weapon nearby—not to destroy the asteroid, but to nudge it just a little bit in a different direction. An early enough push might be enough to shove it off course so it misses Earth.

Another idea is not to push the approaching asteroid at all, but to pull it. By parking a probe or even a smaller asteroid in orbit around an approaching asteroid or comet, the gravitational attraction between the two will slowly move the dangerous NEO off course, saving the planet. This could be the easiest and least dangerous option of the three.

While an asteroid impact is possible, it's not very likely. And, if a space rock was on a collision course with Earth, it's probable we could do something about it given enough time. However, another type of threat that we've known about for years might be harder to stop than a speeding asteroid—the changing climate on Earth.

On February 15, 2013, an asteroid about 65 feet wide exploded in the air over the Russian city of Chelyabinsk. The shockwave from the explosion injured about 1,200 people and shattered windows for miles around. You can watch video of the event here!

Meteor Hits
Russia Tuvix72

# CLIMATE CHANGE

It's a fact that Earth is getting warmer. Countless data from satellites, ice cores, tree rings, and other records show that we're living on a quickly warming planet. Ever since Earth formed, the planet has gone through changes in climate. The last ice age ended just 7,000 years ago, with glaciers and ice caps retreating to the poles. Most shifts in climate are the result of tiny changes in Earth's orbit, while a few were caused by large volcanic eruptions or crashing asteroids.

> The warming we're experiencing today is different from any other in the history of the planet, because we have caused it.

Since the beginning of the Industrial Revolution in the late eighteenth century, the average global temperature has increased 1.6 degrees Fahrenheit (0.9 degrees Celsius), most of it occurring in the last 35 years. Nearly all the warming comes from the burning of fossil fuels, such as oil, gas, and coal, which release greenhouse gases, including carbon dioxide, into the air. Although carbon dioxide makes up less than 1 percent of the atmosphere, it's so good at trapping the sun's heat that even a small amount of it is enough to raise the planet's temperature.

Across the globe, the effects of climate change can already be seen. Glaciers and Arctic ice are melting at incredible rates. Ocean and atmospheric temperatures are rising, and rapidly changing environments are making it hard for organisms, even people, to adapt. Severe events such as hurricanes, floods, and forest fires are becoming more common as weather patterns change.

This asteroid, 243 Ida, is about 36 miles long and even has its own mini moon!

Credit: NASA/JPL

A changing climate means higher sea levels and a greater chance for flooding, as seen on Assateague Island on the East Coast of the United States.

Today, climate scientists are focused on keeping the planet from getting too warm. The Paris Climate Agreement aims to keep temperatures from rising more than 3.6 degrees Fahrenheit (2 degrees Celsius) by the end of the century. To do this, countries will need to sharply reduce the amount of greenhouse gases they emit—and soon. If not, Earth could get even hotter, making it impossible to live in some places.

Although climate change won't destroy Earth, it will dramatically change parts of the planet and could make some of them uninhabitable. If people around the world work together, we might be able to stop the worst of the effects of climate change from happening. However, in the very distant future, a very different kind of climate change will occur—and we cannot do anything to stop it.

## THE END OF THE SUN

When talking about the eventual end of the sun, there's good news and there's bad news. The good news is that the sun is only about halfway through its 10-billion-year life cycle, and astronomers estimate we've got about 5.5 billion years to go before it becomes a white dwarf. The bad news is that it'll make Earth an impossible place to live a little sooner than that.

Since it was born, the sun has slowly become brighter as it works its way through its hydrogen fuel. About 1 billion years from now, the sun will be 10 percent brighter than it is today. This small change in luminosity might not sound like much, but it will be more than enough to bake the Earth and make it much too hot for anything to live on its surface. Humans have no way to stop this catastrophic change, and it's only going to get worse. In 3 to 4 billion years, the sun will be 40-percent brighter, boiling away all of Earth's oceans and turning our home into a hellish, Venus-like world.

Speaking of Venus, around 5.4 billion years from now, the sun will start its red giant phase, swelling in size and swallowing both Mercury and Venus. From Earth, the giant red sun will look as if it fills the entire sky—though nothing on Earth will be alive to see it. The thick atmosphere of Earth's Venus-like phase will be long gone, the planet stripped bare and baked dry by the intense radiation of the bloated sun. Even if humans moved onto Mars, their second home will eventually become an airless, overcooked world, too.

As the sun erupts and throws off its outer layers, anything icy in the asteroid belt will probably melt. As the sun loses mass, its gravitational pull will weaken and the outer planets will drift farther away. A planet or two might even be tossed into interstellar space. Any ring systems will be vaporized and blown away in the blistering solar wind. Icy moons such as Europa might melt and even become small water worlds wrapped in dense atmosphere. But they, too, will eventually be baked dry by the growing solar inferno. Even the most distant worlds— such as Pluto—will feel the heat.

## WEATHER OR CLIMATE?

People often confuse weather and climate, which are different. Weather is what happens in the atmosphere at a particular place and time. For example, a weather report for the Sonoran Desert might predict rain tomorrow. Climate, however, is what the weather is like in an area during a long period of time. While it might just rain in the Sonoran Desert tomorrow, its climate is hot and dry. Climate is what you expect the weather to be like, while the weather is what actually happens.

The sun will eventually burn away Earth's atmosphere.

By the time the sun finally becomes a white dwarf, the solar system will be dramatically different. Any future humans living on planets around distant stars would find the old neighborhood unrecognizable and probably not worth a visit.

## MILKY WAY COLLISION!

During the next few billion years, our solar system won't be the only thing to change. As the sun continues to grow slowly brighter on its way to becoming a red giant, the Milky Way as we know it will be coming to an end.

About 2.5 billion years from now, the members of the Local Group of galaxies will start to merge with each other. First, the Magellanic Clouds and a few other nearby dwarf galaxies will be absorbed into the Milky Way, creating a burst of new stars as clouds of gas and dust mix and combine. These galactic fender-benders are nothing compared to what comes next.

An illustration of the Milky Way Galaxy and the Andromeda Galaxy colliding

Credit: NASA; ESA; Z. Levay and R. van der Marel, STScI; T. Hallas; and A. Mellinger

Right now, the Andromeda Galaxy is barreling toward the Milky Way at more than 248,500 miles per hour. Thankfully, the two galaxies are separated by 2.5 million light years—but that distance is closing fast. About 4.5 billion years from now, Andromeda will collide with the Milky Way in a fireworks display of galactic proportions.

Their collision will cause massive bursts of star formation as clouds of dust and gas from both galaxies mix and collapse. As more time passes, the two galaxies will slowly spiral together, merging into a giant elliptical galaxy scientists have nicknamed Milkdromeda.

But the dramatic stellar lightshow comes at a price. Almost all the gas and dust will be used up in the collision, making the brief, brilliant burst of new stars the last big, star-forming event in either galaxy.

During the next 100 to 200 billion years, Milkdromeda will grow a little larger, gradually pulling in and merging with the rest of the Local Group galaxies. By then, most stars, including the sun, will have long since burned out. Only tiny red dwarfs will still shine, and the massive galaxy will gradually fade as the red dwarfs run out of fuel.

> The final, absolute fate of Milkdromeda and whatever remains of our solar system depends on the ultimate fate of the universe.

## UNIVERSE'S END

How will the universe end? We know that the universe is expanding in all directions, growing larger and cooler as time moves ahead. But will it expand forever?

For a long time, cosmologists suspected that the combined gravitational pull of all matter in the universe was enough to gradually slow and reverse its expansion. Billions of years in the future, distant galaxies would stop moving away from each other and start to creep closer together.

Could the sun collide with another star when the Milky Way and Andromeda galaxies collide? Probably not! Although both galaxies contain hundreds of billions of stars, they're separated by huge amounts of empty space. The chance of a single star or planet colliding with another is  extremely low! Check out this simulation of the galactic pileup here!

vimeo sciencecast titanic collision

Having cooled since the Big Bang, the universe would finally start to warm as energy is squeezed into a shrinking amount of space. As the pace quickens, galaxies would blend into giant mega galaxies, and even those would grow larger until everything in the observable universe came together to make one gigantic collection of an uncountable number of stars. But, as the temperature of space grows hotter, stars and planets would cook in place and eventually explode.

Finally, it would be too much for even atoms to exist, and all the matter and energy in the universe would collapse into an immeasurably hot and dense singularity, like a reverse Big Bang called the Big Crunch.

However, at the end of the twentieth century, cosmologists discovered something unexpected. The expansion of the universe isn't slowing down, it's speeding up. Some strange, unknown force is fighting against the gravity of the entire universe, pushing apart galaxies at a faster and faster rate.

## DARK ENERGY

To beat back the gravitational pull of the entire universe, you need an incredible amount of energy. And, looking around the universe today, you'd probably think it's mostly made of matter.

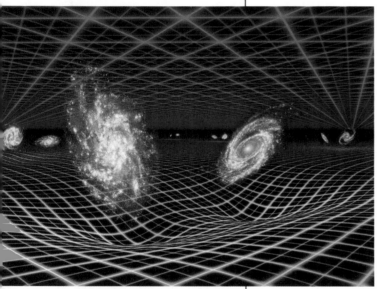

In this artist's conception, dark energy is represented by the purple grid above and gravity by the green grid below.

Credit: NASA/JPL-Caltech

After all, billions of galaxies are found in all directions, each filled with millions or even trillions of stars and planets. Surprisingly, that's not the case. Ordinary matter, such as you and your friends, Earth, and anything else made of atoms, makes up less than 5 percent of the entire universe. Invisible dark matter, whatever it is, makes up only 27 percent. For the universe's expansion to be speeding up, 68 percent of the cosmos must be made of some mysterious, invisible energy pushing the universe apart.

Cosmologists call it dark energy.

As with dark matter, nobody really knows what dark energy is or how it works. It could be a strange kind of energy woven into the fabric of space itself, growing stronger as more space fills the cosmos between galaxies. Dark energy could also come from space itself. We usually think of space as being empty, but it's full of short-lived particles that pop into and out of existence like a barely detectable hum of matter and energy across the universe. These temporary, or "virtual," particles could be supplying the universe with its dark energy. So far, nobody has figured out a way to test these ideas.

Possibly, dark energy isn't real at all, and it's our understanding of gravity that's wrong. But the theory of gravity explains so well why rockets, black holes, and home runs work, that it's hard to imagine we've had gravity wrong this whole time!

Whatever dark energy is or is not, its effect on the universe is real. By pushing the universe apart at an ever-increasing pace, cosmologists are sure we won't end up in a Big Crunch. It's much more likely that the universe will end up as a cold, dark void—the Big Freeze.

## COSMIC CONCEPT

More than 95 percent of the universe is made of mysterious dark energy and dark matter.

## THE BIG RIP

If dark energy grows in strength, the expansion of the universe could turn violent. After all the distant galaxies are carried away, the expansion of space would affect the galaxies themselves, tearing stars away from each other before shredding them and their planets to their atoms. Finally, dark energy could overcome all the forces of nature and even rip atoms and their building blocks apart, leaving the universe empty of all matter. The Big Rip isn't likely, but scientists haven't ruled it out completely.

## TEXT TO WORLD

What evidence of climate change do you notice where you live? Are storms more severe? Do you live where fire is a major threat?

The most likely end of the universe is a cold, dark sleep. If the cosmos continues to expand and cool, galaxies will continue to fade from view, carried away by the stretching of space. One to 2 trillion years from now, Milkdromeda will be the only galaxy left in our observable universe. During the next 100 trillion years, even Milkdromeda will fade as its last stars grow dim and become cold black dwarfs. In that far future, the universe will become truly dark.

Eventually, almost all matter will be swallowed up by supermassive black holes, the only remnants of galaxies in the universe. But even these monsters will gradually fade away. In the almost immeasurable distant future, the entire universe will cool to just above absolute zero, the coldest possible temperature in the universe. No usable energy will be left and no life will be able to survive.

*If the Big Freeze is the universe's ultimate fate, not everything is lost.*

In a cosmos with nothing left but time, nothing is impossible. At some point, a new universe could pop into existence, starting with a new Big Bang.

Fortunately, the end of the universe is a long way off. We have plenty of time to keep studying and improving our understanding of life, Earth, stars, galaxies, and the universe itself.

### KEY QUESTIONS

- **What are some ways researchers can test theories that might not be proved until billions of years into the future?**
- **What actions can people take on a daily basis to combat climate change?**

# LEAVING EARTH

Earth is a wonderful place, but it won't be habitable forever. Lots of science fiction stories send humanity off to other planets and moons to escape the eventual death of the sun. With the discovery of exoplanets such as TRAPPIST-1e, we might have a few places to move to when the time comes—but it wouldn't be easy!

- **Research a new home for humanity.** Where could we go? We've found thousands of exoplanets, but only a few might have the right conditions for life. You can start checking out possible new homes at this website.

 NASA visions future

- **How would we get to this new home?** Do we currently have the technology to travel to another star system? What technologies do we need? How long would it take to reach our destination?

- **What would life be like on our new home planet?** Would humans need to evolve to fit into their new world? What kind of adaptations would be beneficial for the world you chose?

> To investigate more, consider other options that might exist besides moving humanity to a new star system. Can we live on spacecraft, forever traveling through space? What other solutions can you think of?

### Inquire & Investigate

## VOCAB LAB

Write down what you think each word means. What root words can you find to help you? What does the context of the word tell you?

**Big Crunch**, **Big Freeze**, **climate**, **climate change**, **dark energy**, **near-Earth objects (NEOs)**, and **weather**.

Compare your definitions with those of your friends or classmates. Did you all come up with the same meanings? Turn to the text and glossary if you need help.

# Inquire & Investigate

## CLIMATE CHANGE

Earth's climate is changing drastically, but it's not too late to do something about it. Around the world, countries have signed on to the Paris Agreement to limit and reduce the worst effects of climate change. You can also do your part at home!

Around the world, people are getting involved in climate activism. Greta Thunberg (2003– ), a Swedish teenager and climate activist, has been nominated for the Nobel Peace Prize for her work—twice! You can learn more about her and her work here!

🔍 Greta Thunberg facts

- **Come up with a plan to reduce your carbon footprint.** Your carbon footprint is the amount of carbon dioxide that's released into the air by your use of energy. It can be affected by how you get around, how you use electricity, and even how you shop. To help understand how you can reduce your carbon footprint, check out this website.

🔍 reduce your carbon footprint, hot mess

- **Try some of these climate-friendly options!**

  - Walk or share rides when you need to go somewhere

  - Eat locally grown food

  - Research power options based on renewable energies such as wind and solar. Are these right for your home or school?

  - Use reusable bags when shopping

  - Attend a climate march to help raise awareness of the issue in your own community

- **How else could you help?**

> To investigate more, research a green career—saving the world from climate change isn't just for scientists. What kinds of green careers might you be interested in and why?

**abiogenesis:** the beginning of life from non-living things.

**absorb:** to soak up a liquid or take in energy, heat, light, or sound.

**accretion disk:** a flat, spinning disk of matter surrounding a massive object such as a star, planet, or black hole.

**active galactic nuclei (AGN):** a small, bright region at a galaxy's center containing a supermassive black hole.

**adapt:** to make a change in response to new or different conditions.

**algae:** a plant-like organism that turns light into energy but does not have leaves or roots.

**alien:** something strange, unfamiliar, or new, such as an alien life form or planet.

**amino acid:** an organic compound that serves as a building block for proteins.

**ancestor:** someone from your family who lived before you.

**annihilate:** to destroy totally.

**antimatter:** atoms or matter formed by antiparticles.

**antiparticle:** a subatomic particle with the opposite electrical charge of a regular subatomic particle twin.

**antiproton:** a particle identical to a proton except with a negative electrical charge.

**archaea:** a class of prokaryotes that often live in extreme environments.

**asteroid:** a small rocky object that orbits the sun.

**asteroid belt:** a region in space between Mars and Jupiter that contains many asteroids.

**astrobiologist:** a scientist who studies the possibility of life beyond Earth.

**astronomical unit (AU):** a unit of distance defined as the average distance between Earth and the sun, about 93 million miles.

**astronomy:** the study of planets, stars, galaxies, and everything else in the universe. An astronomer studies astronomy.

**atmosphere:** the mixture of gases that surround a planet.

**atom:** a small piece of matter, made of protons and neutrons orbited by electrons.

**atomic:** about or relating to atoms.

**atomic reaction:** a process that changes the nucleus of an atom, such as nuclear fusion.

**Australopithecine:** an extinct human ancestor that lived 1–4 million years ago.

**axial tilt:** the angle between a planet's axis and the plane of its orbit.

**axis:** an imaginary line around which an object rotates.

**bacteria:** microorganisms found in air, soil, water, plants, and animals that are often beneficial but sometimes harmful.

**barred spiral:** a spiral galaxy with a dense, bar-shaped collection of stars running through its nucleus.

**BCE:** put after a date, BCE stands for Before Common Era and counts down to zero. CE stands for Common Era and counts up from zero. These nonreligious terms correspond to BC and AD. This book was printed in 2021 CE.

**Big Bang:** the theory that the universe began in an incredibly hot and dense state and suddenly began to expand everywhere in all directions.

**Big Bang nucleosynthesis:** the formation of the first atomic nuclei in the universe, beginning about 10 seconds after the Big Bang.

**Big Crunch:** a possible future of the universe in which everything collapses back into a hot, dense singularity.

**Big Freeze:** a possible future of the universe where space expands forever and everything cools to absolute zero (0 kelvin).

**binary star system:** two stars orbiting a common center of gravity.

**biology:** the study of life and living things.

**biome:** a natural area with a distinct climate and with plants and animals adapted for life there. Deserts and rainforests are examples of biomes.

**biosphere:** the part of Earth's crust, waters, and atmosphere that supports life.

**bipedal:** using only two limbs for walking.

**black dwarf:** a dead star that no longer emits light or heat. The final stage of most stars in the universe.

# GLOSSARY

**black hole:** an object so massive that it collapses under its own gravity. Nothing, not even light, can escape.

**blue supergiant:** the biggest and hottest type of main sequence star.

**brown dwarf:** a failed star that never grows large enough to shine by nuclear fusion.

**Cambrian Explosion:** a massive increase in the diversity of life on Earth that happened about 540 million years ago.

**carbon dioxide:** a combination of carbon and oxygen that is formed by the burning of fossil fuels, the rotting of plants and animals, and the breathing out of animals or humans.

**carbon footprint:** the total amount of carbon dioxide and other greenhouse gases emitted during the full life cycle of a product or service or by a person or family in a year.

**cell:** the basic part of a living thing. Cells are so small they can be seen with only a microscope. There are billions of cells in most living things.

**chemistry:** the science of how atoms and molecules combine to form substances and how those substances interact, combine, and change.

**chromosphere:** a thin, hot layer of the sun's atmosphere just above the photosphere.

**citizen science:** the involvement of everyday people in scientific activities or projects.

**civilization:** a community of people with a highly developed culture and social organization that is advanced in art, science, and government.

**climate:** the weather patterns in an area during a long period of time.

**climate change:** a change in long-term weather patterns, which can happen through natural or manmade processes.

**comet:** a ball of ice and dust that orbits the sun.

**compressed:** pressed together very tightly so something takes up less space.

**condense:** to change from a gas to a liquid.

**constellation:** a group of stars that form a recognizable shape or pattern.

**convection:** the transfer of heat from one region to another by the movement of a gas or liquid.

**convective zone:** an interior layer of the sun where energy travels by convection.

**core:** the center of an object.

**corona:** the incredibly hot outermost part of the sun's atmosphere.

**coronal mass ejections (CMEs):** gigantic bubbles of hot plasma and radiation that explode from the sun's surface and can travel through the solar system with tremendous speed.

**cosmic inflation:** the rapid expansion of space that occurred just after the Big Bang.

**cosmic microwave background radiation:** the theory that the universe is filled with radiation that is leftover heat from the Big Bang.

**cosmic radiation:** high-energy particles that move through space at nearly the speed of light.

**cosmology:** the science of the origin and development of the universe. A cosmologist studies cosmology.

**cosmos:** the universe seen as a well-ordered whole.

**creation myth:** a story about how life, Earth, or the universe was created. Creation myths are found in nearly every culture.

**crust:** the solid, outermost layer of a rocky planet.

**culture:** the beliefs and way of life of a group of people, which can include religion, language, art, clothing, food, holidays, tools, and more.

**cyanobacteria:** a blue-green type of aquatic bacteria that produces oxygen through photosynthesis.

**dark energy:** an unknown form of energy that seems to make up 68 percent of the universe. It is thought to cause space to expand faster and faster through time.

**dark matter:** a type of matter that interacts with regular matter only through gravity.

**debris:** the scattered pieces of something that has been broken or destroyed.

**debunk:** to expose as false.

**decay:** to break down.

**Denisovan:** a close relative of modern humans that went extinct around 30,000 to 40,000 years ago.

**dense:** tightly packed together.

**density wave:** a wave of gas and dust that travels through a galaxy's disk and is thought to create spiral arms.

**differentiate:** the separation of an object's internal structure by its physical or chemical makeup.

**diverse:** a large variety of people or things.

**DNA:** stands for deoxyribonucleic acid. The substance found in your cells that carries your genetic information, the blueprint of who you are.

**doctrine:** a set of beliefs held by a group.

**dominant:** stronger or more powerful than another.

**dust lane:** dark clouds of interstellar dust that block the light of stars behind them.

**dwarf galaxy:** a small galaxy with only a few hundred million or billion stars, often found orbiting larger galaxies.

**dwarf planet:** a small, round object that circles the sun but has not cleared its orbit of other dwarf planets.

**eclipse:** the passing of one body in space, such as the moon, into the shadow of another.

**ecosystem:** an interdependent community of living and non-living things and their environment.

**electromagnetic force:** a fundamental force of nature that is responsible for electricity, magnetism, and light.

**electromagnetic radiation:** a form of energy that moves through space, such as radio waves, gamma rays, and visible light.

**electromagnetic spectrum:** the entire range of electromagnetic radiation that includes high-energy cosmic rays and gamma rays, X-rays, radio waves, short microwaves, ultraviolet and infrared light, and visible light.

**electron:** a particle in an atom with a negative charge that moves around the nucleus.

**element:** a basic substance, such as gold or oxygen, made of only one kind of atom.

**elementary particle:** the smallest parts of matter in the universe, such as quarks and gluons.

**elliptical:** shaped like an ellipse, or an oval.

**elliptical galaxy:** large, elliptical-shaped galaxies that do not have spiral arms.

**embryo:** something in its early stages of development.

**emit:** to send or give out something, such as smoke, gas, heat, or light.

**energy:** the ability to do things, to work.

**engineer:** a person who uses science, math, and creativity to design and build things.

**epicycle:** a small circle whose center moves around the circumference of a larger one.

**equator:** an imaginary line around the middle of the earth that divides it in two halves.

**eukaryote:** a class of organisms composed of one or more cells that contain a nucleus.

**evaporate:** to change from a liquid to a gas, or vapor.

**event horizon:** the theoretical edge of a black hole, past which nothing can escape.

**evidence:** something that proves, or could prove, the existence of something or the truth of an idea.

**evolution:** the process by which a species changes through generations due to mutation and natural selection.

**evolve:** to change or develop slowly, during long periods of time.

**exoplanet:** a planet that orbits a star other than the sun.

**exosphere:** a very thin layer of gas surrounding a planet.

**expand:** to spread out and take up more space.

**extinction:** the death of an entire species so that it no longer exists.

**force:** a push or a pull that causes a change of motion in an object.

**fossil:** the remains of any organism, including animals and plants, that have been preserved in rock.

**fossil fuel:** a natural fuel that formed long ago from the remains of living organisms. Oil, natural gas, and coal are fossil fuels.

# GLOSSARY

**friction:** a force that slows down objects when they contact each other. Friction acts in opposition to movement.

**fundamental forces of nature:** four forces that determine how matter and energy interact within the universe—gravity, the electromagnetic force, the strong nuclear force, and the weak nuclear force.

**fuse:** to join.

**galactic:** having to do with a galaxy.

**galactic halo:** a large collection of gas, dust, ancient stars, and dark matter surrounding the Milky Way.

**galaxy:** a very large collection of stars, gas, and dust held together by gravity. Earth is in a galaxy called the Milky Way.

**gamma ray:** light that has the shortest wavelength and highest energy.

**gas giant:** a huge planet made mostly of hydrogen and helium.

**general relativity:** the theory that gravity warps space and time, proposed by Albert Einstein.

**genetic:** traits that are passed from parent to child in DNA.

**geocentric:** a model of the universe, now disproved, that Earth is the center of the solar system.

**geosphere:** the region of Earth that includes everything from the rocky crust to the liquid core.

**glacier:** a huge mass of ice and snow.

**gluon:** a particle that helps bind quarks together to form protons and neutrons.

**gravitational pull:** a force of nature that causes every mass, or object, to exert a force on every other object.

**gravity:** a fundamental force of nature that pulls all objects with mass or energy together.

**greenhouse effect:** a process through which energy from the sun is trapped by a planet's atmosphere, warming the planet.

**greenhouse gas:** a gas in the atmosphere that traps heat. We need some greenhouse gases, but too much traps too much heat and causes climate change.

**habitable zone:** the distance from a star at which liquid water could exist on a planet's surface.

**heliocentric:** a disproved model of the universe with the sun at the center, circled by the planets and stars.

**helium:** a colorless gas created in a nuclear reaction in the sun. It is the most common element in the universe after hydrogen.

**helium flash:** the rapid fusing of a star's helium core into heavier elements near the end of its main sequence.

**Homo erectus:** an extinct hominin species that lived in Africa and Eurasia between 1.9 million and 100,000 years ago.

**Homo habilis:** the earliest known human ancestor, who lived between 1 and 2.5 million years ago.

**Homo neanderthalensis:** an extinct hominin species that lived in Europe and Asia between 400,000 and 28,000 years ago. This species is considered to be the closest relative to *Homo sapiens*.

**Homo sapiens:** the Latin words meaning "wise man" for the species of all living human beings today.

**homogenous:** the same.

**hydrogen:** the simplest and most abundant element in the universe. Hydrogen and oxygen are the two elements in water.

**hydrologic cycle:** a continuous process of water moving between Earth and its atmosphere through evaporation, condensation, and precipitation.

**hydrosphere:** all the Earth's water, including oceans, rivers, lakes, glaciers, and water vapor in the air.

**ice age:** a period of time when ice covers a large part of Earth.

**ice core:** a sample of ice taken out of a glacier, used to study climate.

**ideology:** a set of opinions or beliefs.

**Industrial Revolution:** a period during the eighteenth and nineteenth centuries when large cities and factories began to replace small towns and farming.

**infinite:** limitless or endless and impossible to measure or calculate.

**inner core:** the innermost layer of Earth, made of super-hot solid metal.

**interbreed:** to mate with each other and have children.

**International Space Station (ISS):** a massive space station orbiting Earth where astronauts live, conduct experiments, and study space.

**interstellar:** existing or occurring between stars.

**irregular galaxy:** a smaller galaxy with no obvious shape or structure.

**kinetic impaction:** the use of a fast-moving object to slam into and change the course of an asteroid or a comet.

**law of universal gravitation:** Sir Isaac Newton's theory of gravity, which says that gravity is a force that pulls all matter together and depends on each object's mass and distance.

**lenticular galaxy:** a galaxy that has features of both elliptical and spiral galaxies.

**light year:** a unit of measure for very long distances. One light year is how far light travels in a year, about 6 trillion miles (9.5 trillion kilometers).

**lithium:** the third most abundant element in the universe after hydrogen and helium.

**Local Group:** a large collection of about 50 nearby galaxies, including the Milky Way and Andromeda galaxies.

**luminosity:** the total amount of energy emitted by a star.

**magma:** hot, melted rock below Earth's surface.

**magnetic field:** the area around a magnetic object, such as a magnet or a planet, that exerts a magnetic force.

**main sequence star:** a star that is fusing hydrogen atoms into helium atoms in its core. It is a star's longest stage of life.

**mammal:** a type of animal, such as a human, dog, or cat. Mammals are born live, feed milk to their young, and usually have hair or fur covering most of their skin.

**mantle:** the layer of a terrestrial planet, such as Earth, between the crust and core.

**mass:** the amount of matter in an object.

**mass extinction:** a period in Earth's history when very large numbers of species die out in a short period of time.

**massive compact halo objects (MACHOs):** massive objects surrounding galaxies that are hard to detect, such as small black holes or brown dwarfs. One possible explanation for dark matter.

**matter:** anything that has weight and takes up space.

**mesosphere:** the atmosphere above the stratosphere.

**meteorite:** a piece of rock from space that lands on Earth.

**microorganism:** a living thing so small that it can be seen only with a microscope.

**microwave:** electromagnetic radiation with a wavelength between visible light and radio waves.

**migration:** moving from one place to another.

**Milky Way:** the large, barred spiral galaxy that our solar system calls home.

**mineral:** a naturally occurring solid found in rocks and in the ground. Rocks are made of minerals. Gold and diamonds are precious minerals.

**molecule:** a group of two or more atoms bound together.

**molten:** made liquid by heat.

**multicellular organism:** an organism with two or more cells.

**mutation:** a permanent change in an organism's DNA.

**natural selection:** the process that allows organisms best adapted for an environment to reproduce and pass their useful traits to their offspring.

**Neanderthal:** a close relative of modern humans that went extinct around 30,000 to 40,000 years ago.

**near-Earth objects (NEOs):** asteroids or comets with orbits that take them near Earth.

**nebula:** a giant cloud of gas and dust where stars and solar systems form. Plural is nebulae.

**neutron:** a subatomic particle with no charge that, when combined with protons, forms the nucleus of atoms.

**neutron star:** a star that has collapsed under its gravity and whose atoms have all converted to neutrons.

**nuclear:** relating to energy coming from the center of an atom, called the nucleus.

**nuclear fusion:** a nuclear reaction that combines smaller atoms to form larger atoms, releasing huge amounts of energy. It is the power source of all stars.

# GLOSSARY

**nuclear weapon:** a powerful weapon that uses the energy released by the splitting of atoms.

**nucleus:** the center of an object, including atoms and galaxies. Plural is nuclei.

**nutrient:** a substance an organism needs to live and grow.

**observable universe:** the part of the universe we can actually see and detect, beyond which light hasn't had enough time to reach us yet. It is about 93 billion light-years wide.

**opaque:** not transparent.

**orbit:** the path an object in space takes around a star, planet, or moon due to gravity.

**organelle:** a structure within a cell that has a special function.

**organic:** something that is or was living, such as animals, wood, grass, and insects.

**organism:** a living thing, such as an animal or a plant.

**outer core:** a spinning mix of liquid nickel and iron surrounding Earth's inner core.

**oxygen:** a gas in the air that animals and humans need to breathe to stay alive.

**ozone layer:** the layer in the stratosphere that absorbs most of the sun's ultraviolet radiation.

**paleontology:** the study of the history of life on Earth through fossils of plants and animals.

**panspermia:** a theory that life began elsewhere in the universe and was brought to Earth.

**particle:** a very small bit of matter such as a molecule, atom, or electron.

**particle accelerator:** a machine that propels particles to high speeds for use in basic research in particle physics.

**periodic table:** a chart that shows the chemical elements arranged according to their properties.

**philosophy:** the study of truth, wisdom, the nature of reality, and knowledge.

**photon:** a particle of light.

**photosphere:** the brightest, most visible layer of a star, what we see as the surface.

**photosynthesis:** the process plants use to turn sunlight, carbon dioxide, and water into food.

**physics:** the science of matter, energy, and forces in the universe and how they interact with each other. A physicist studies physics.

**planetary nebula:** a glowing shell of gas and dust ejected from a dying star.

**planetesimal:** a small object formed early in the solar system that could go on to form a planet.

**plasma:** a state of matter similar to a gas, but with temperatures and pressures so high that electrons are stripped away from their atoms and move freely. It is the most common form of matter in the universe.

**precipitation:** falling moisture in the form of rain, sleet, snow, or hail.

**pressure:** a force that pushes on an object.

**primate:** a mammal belonging to a classification order including humans that shares the following features: a large brain, opposable thumbs, good eyesight, and flexible toes.

**primeval atom:** physicist Georges Lemaître's description of the early universe, what would later become known as the Big Bang.

**probe:** a spaceship or satellite used to explore outer space.

**prokaryote:** a single-celled organism that lacks a nucleus.

**protein:** an organic molecule found in all living plants and animals that provides the major structural and functional components of cells.

**protogalaxy:** a small collection of gas, dust, and stars that grow to become galaxies.

**proton:** a subatomic particle with a positive charge that, when combined with neutrons, forms the nucleus of atoms.

**protoplanet:** a large body of matter in orbit around the sun or a star and thought to be developing into a planet.

**protostar:** an early stage of a star's evolution, when a contracting ball of hot gas and dust has not yet reached the mass needed to start nuclear fusion.

**Ptolemaic system:** a disproved model of the universe that places Earth at the center.

**pulsar:** a rapidly spinning neutron star that emits beams of radio waves. It appears to pulse when those beams point toward Earth.

**quark-gluon plasma:** a hot and dense state of matter in the early universe, when it was too hot for quarks and gluons to form larger particles.

**quark:** an elementary particle that combines with gluons to form protons, neutrons, and other subatomic particles. The smallest piece of matter in the universe.

**quasar:** an object in space that emits huge amounts of energy.

**radial velocity method:** a method of detecting exoplanets by measuring how their gravity effects their star's motion.

**radiation:** energy that travels through space as waves and particles.

**radiative zone:** the layer surrounding the sun's core where energy created during nuclear fusion travels by radiation.

**radio wave:** an electromagnetic wave used to transmit radio and television signals and for navigation.

**red dwarf:** the smallest, coolest, and longest-shining stars in the universe.

**red giant:** a cool, red, and hugely swollen star that has left its main sequence and is near the end of its life.

**reflect:** to redirect something that hits a surface, such as heat, light, or sound.

**retrograde motion:** rotating in the opposite direction than normal.

**satellite:** an object that orbits a larger object in space.

**simulation:** a virtual environment that looks, feels, and behaves like the real world.

**singularity:** the center of a black hole, where matter is thought to be infinitely dense.

**skepticism:** doubting the truth of something.

**solar cycle:** the 11-year cycle of magnetic activity of the sun.

**solar flare:** a sudden burst of radiation from the sun's surface.

**solar maximum:** the peak of the sun's 11-year solar cycle, when its surface and atmosphere are likely to be the most active.

**solar minimum:** the lowest point of the sun's 11-year solar cycle, when its surface and atmosphere are likely to be the least active.

**solar prominence:** a huge loop of super-hot plasma extending from the sun's surface.

**solar system:** the collection of eight planets and their moons in orbit around the sun, together with smaller bodies in the form of asteroids, meteoroids, comets, and dwarf planets.

**solar wind:** the flow of electrically charged particles from the sun.

**species:** a class of organisms having common characteristics or qualities.

**spectral type:** a system used by astronomers to classify stars based on their color and surface temperature.

**spectrograph:** an instrument used to study the properties of light by splitting it into different wavelengths.

**spectrum:** a band of colors that a ray of light can be separated into to measure properties of the object, including motion and composition.

**speed of light:** the speed at which light travels through space, which is 186,000 miles per second.

**sphere:** a round shape that looks like a ball.

**spiral:** winding in a continuous and gradually widening or tightening curve.

**spiral arm:** a collection of gas, dust, and young stars twisting out and away from a spiral galaxy's center.

**spiral galaxy:** a disk-shaped galaxy with spiral arms that twist out and away from its center.

**stellar black hole:** a black hole formed after the collapse of a star that is at least 20 times more massive than the sun.

**stratosphere:** the middle region of the atmosphere, where the ozone layer is.

**stromatolites:** the oldest known fossils, first created by blue-green algae in ancient seas more than 3 billion years ago.

**strong nuclear force:** a fundamental force of nature that holds together the particles that make up atoms.

**sunspot:** a dark area on the sun's surface that is cooler than the surrounding area.

**super-Earth:** an exoplanet with a mass greater than Earth but less than Neptune.

# GLOSSARY

**supermassive black hole:** the largest type of black hole, with masses greater than a million sun-like stars.

**supernatural:** beings, objects, or events that cannot be explained by science.

**supernova:** a powerful explosion at the end of a large star's life.

**symbiotic:** having an interdependent relationship.

**technology:** the tools, methods, and systems used to solve a problem or do work.

**tectonic plates:** large slabs of the earth's crust that are in constant motion. The plates move on the mantle, the hot, melted layer below the crust.

**terrain:** the physical features of land.

**terrestrial planet:** an Earth-like planet with a rocky surface.

**tetrapod:** a vertebrate with two pairs of limbs, such as an amphibian, bird, or mammal.

**theoretician:** in physics, someone who uses math to make models and predictions, rather than using actual experiments.

**theory:** an idea that tries to explain why something is the way it is based on facts.

**thermosphere:** the hottest part of the atmosphere, rising more than 300 miles above the surface of Earth.

**trait:** a characteristic.

**transit:** the blocking of a small amount of light from a star by a small object, such as a planet.

**transit method:** a method of detecting exoplanets by measuring the small changes in a star's light as the exoplanet passes between it and Earth.

**troposphere:** the lowest part of Earth's atmosphere, where most weather occurs.

**tundra:** a cold, mostly treeless area in very northern and very southern latitudes.

**turbulence:** violent movement.

**universal gravitation:** Newton's law that states all objects in the universe experience gravity.

**ultraviolet radiation:** high-energy radiation that can cause sunburns.

**universe:** everything that exists, everywhere.

**unprecedented:** never done or known before.

**velocity:** the speed of an object in a particular direction.

**vertebrate:** an organism with a backbone or spinal column.

**water vapor:** the gas form of water in the air.

**weather:** local temperature, cloudiness, rainfall, and wind.

**white dwarf:** the final stage of life for a star the size of the sun, when fusion no longer takes place.

**weak nuclear force:** a fundamental force of nature that helps particles to decay by emitting radiation.

**weakly interacting massive particles (WIMPs):** theoretical subatomic particles that interact with matter only through gravity. One possible explanation for dark matter.

**X-ray:** a high-energy electromagnetic wave.

**yellow dwarf:** a common, medium-sized star such as the sun.

# RESOURCES

## BOOKS

DK, *Super Earth Encyclopedia*. DK Children, 2017.

Sutter, Paul M. *Your Place in the Universe: Understanding Our Big, Messy Existence*. Prometheus, 2018.

Tyson, Neil deGrasse, and Gregory Mone. *Astrophysics for Young People in a Hurry*. Norton Young Readers, 2019.

# RESOURCES

## WEBSITES

**NASA's SpacePlace - Younger Readers:**
spaceplace.nasa.gov

**The Solar System and Beyond - NASA:**
nasa.gov/topics/solarsystem/index.html

**The Solar System - Interactive - NASA:**
solarsystem.nasa.gov

**Exoplanets - Interactive - NASA:**
exoplanets.nasa.gov

**Center for Near-Earth Objects - JPL/NASA:**
cneos.jpl.nasa.gov/about/basics.html

**Climate Change for Kids - NASA:**
climatekids.nasa.gov

**National Geographic Resource Library:**
nationalgeographic.org/education/resource-library/?q=&page=1&per_page=25

**Smithsonian National Museum of Natural History:**
humanorigins.si.edu

## SELECTED BIBLIOGRAPHY

Ryden, Barbara. *Introduction to Cosmology* (2nd Edition). Cambridge University Press, 2016.

Sutter, Paul M. *Your Place in the Universe: Understanding Our Big, Messy Existence*. Prometheus, 2018.

**The Smithsonian Institution's Human Origins Program:**
humanorigins.si.edu

**NASA:**
nasa.gov

**NASA Science - Solar System Exploration:**
solarsystem.nasa.gov/planets/overview

**NASA Science - Planets Beyond Our Solar System:**
exoplanets.nasa.gov

**National Geographic Resource Library:**
nationalgeographic.org/education/resource-library

**EarthHow:**
earthhow.com

Siegel, Ethan, Brian Koberlein, Jillian Scudder. *Starts With A Bang*. forbes.com/sites/startswithabang

# RESOURCES

**page 7:** youtube.com/watch?v=M0p6NKANE08

**page 8:** nytimes.com/1992/10/31/world/after-350-years-vatican-says-galileo-was-right-it-moves.html

**page 9:** youtube.com/watch?v=Yv3EMq2Dgq8&list=PLsNB4peY6C6JDc1HcVKjjYzVB0BYEXexd

**page 16:** youtube.com/watch?v=LraNu_78sCw

**page 17:** ducksters.com/science/periodic_table.php

**page 18:** youtube.com/watch?v=XD8Q3Mb1Q4I

**page 20:** youtube.com/watch?v=jjy-eqWM38g

**page 22:** nasa.gov/mission_pages/webb/main/index.html

**page 31:** jpl.nasa.gov/edu/news/2019/4/19/how-scientists-captured-the-first-image-of-a-black-hole

**page 32:** svs.gsfc.nasa.gov/11534

**page 33:** nasa.gov/jpl/charting-the-milky-way-from-the-inside-out

**page 35:** zooniverse.org/projects/zookeeper/galaxy-zoo

**page 40:** youtube.com/watch?v=ywppy_2M03I

**page 42:** pbs.org/newshour/science/new-3d-maps-of-the-milky-way-confirm-our-galaxy-is-warped

**page 45:** staratlas.com

**page 46:** space.com/18090-alpha-centauri-nearest-star-system.html

**page 47:** youtube.com/watch?v=mZsaaturR6E

**page 51:** youtube.com/watch?time_continue=26&v=SungFXUsoqw

**page 52:** nasa.gov/content/goddard/parker-solar-probe

**page 56:** youtube.com/watch?v=gjLk_72V9Bw

**page 61:** npr.org/2011/02/04/133498152/why-the-former-planet-pluto-got-demoted

**page 61:** findplanetnine.com

**page 63:** solarsystem.nasa.gov/planets/mercury/overview

**page 64:** solarsystem.nasa.gov/planets/venus/overview

**page 65:** solarsystem.nasa.gov/planets/earth/overview

**page 66:** solarsystem.nasa.gov/planets/mars/overview

**page 67:** solarsystem.nasa.gov/planets/jupiter/overview

**page 68:** solarsystem.nasa.gov/planets/saturn/overview

**page 69:** solarsystem.nasa.gov/planets/uranus/overview

**page 70:** solarsystem.nasa.gov/planets/neptune/overview

**page 71:** exoplanets.nasa.gov

**page 72:** solarsystem.nasa.gov/news/335/10-things-all-about-trappist-1

**page 74:** spitzer.caltech.edu/images/6482-ssc2018-04d

**page 74:** spitzer.caltech.edu/images/6479-ssc2018-04c

**page 74:** zooniverse.org/projects/nora-dot-eisner/planet-hunters-tess

**page 83:** youtube.com/watch?v=NNijmxsKGbc

**page 85:** youtube.com/watch?v=P3GagfbA2vo

**page 86:** youtube.com/watch?v=8kK2zwjRV0M

**page 87:** youtube.com/watch?v=Pxujitlv8wc

**page 90:** nationalgeographic.org/projects/out-of-eden-walk

**page 91:** youtube.com/watch?v=DZv8VyIQ7YU

**page 93:** climatekids.nasa.gov/mini-garden

**page 97:** nasa.gov/planetarydefense

**page 97:** nasa.gov/podcasts/on-a-mission

**page 98:** youtube.com/watch?v=dpmXyJrs7iU

**page 103:** vimeo.com/43694515

**page 107:** jpl.nasa.gov/visions-of-the-future

**page 108:** youtube.com/watch?v=KdiA12KeSL0

**page 108:** natgeokids.com/nz/kids-club/cool-kids/general-kids-club/greta-thunberg-facts

# INDEX

# INDEX